Executive Functioning and Young People with ADHD:

Easy Hacks to understand the neurodiverse ADHD mind, get organized, stop procrastination and become independent easily and stress-free

Contents

Introduction 1

Chapter 1: Understanding ADHD and Executive Functioning 4

   1.1 So, What Exactly Is ADHD? 4

   1.2 Executive Functioning: Your Brain's Boss 6

   1.3 Setting the Stage for Success: What's in It for You? 12

Chapter 2: Time Management Techniques for ADHD Legends 14

   2.1 The Pomodoro Technique: Your New Secret Weapon 14

   2.2 Time Blocking: The Art of Owning Your Day 15

   2.3 Time Management Superpowers: Digital Tools Edition 17

   2.4 Daily Routines: The Chill Way to Stay on Track 18

   2.5 Quick Wins: Treat Yo' Self! 19

Chapter 3: Busting Procrastination: Getting Started 21

   3.1 The Two-Minute Rule: Beat Procrastination by Starting Small 21

   3.2 Instant Gratification Techniques: Small Rewards for Big Wins 24

   3.3 Tackling the Worst First: How to Get the Hard Stuff Out of the Way ... 25

   3.4 The Power of Music: Using Playlists to Boost Focus 26

Chapter 4: How to Get Your Life Together Without Losing Your Mind 32

   4.1 Accountability Buddies: Your New Sidekick 32

   4.2 Decluttering: Because Your Room Deserves Better 34

   4.3 The Art of Getting Organized: Make It Fun 35

   4.5 Procrastination-Proofing Your Life 37

   4.5 Your Game Plan for Staying Organized 38

Chapter 5: Emotional Regulation and Mindfulness 39

   5.1 Breathing Hacks: Calm Down Anytime, Anywhere 39

   5.2 Meditation for ADHD Minds: Chill Without the Effort 41

5.3 Journaling: Vent, Reflect, and Reset 41

5.4 The Stress Bucket: Empty It Before It Overflows 42

5.5 Resilience: Your Superpower for Bouncing Back 42

Chapter 6: Boosting Self-Esteem and Building Confidence 43

6.1 Self-Reflection Exercises: Recognizing Your Strengths 43

6.2 Positive Affirmations: Change Your Inner Dialogue, Change Your Life. 46

6.3 Celebrating Small Wins: Why You Shouldn't Skip the Tiny Victories 50

6.4 Peer-Validated Success Stories: Learning from Others 52

6.5 Setting Realistic Goals: Achievable Steps Toward Success 56

Chapter 7: Social Skills and Building Relationships 61

7.1 Reading Social Cues: Tips for Better Understanding Others 61

7.2 Conversation Starters: How to Break the Ice 65

7.3 Maintaining Friendships: The Art of Keeping in Touch 69

7.4 Navigating Social Media: Using Platforms Wisely 73

7.4 Building Your Support Squad: Finding Friends Who Get You 76

Chapter 8: Decision-Making and Prioritization Skills 79

8.1 Decision Fatigue 79

8.2 The Eisenhower Matrix: Prioritizing Tasks Effectively 81

8.3 Making Quick Decisions: Trusting Your Gut 84

8.4 How to Balance School and Social Life Without Losing Your Mind 87

8.5 Dodging Time Traps: How to Crush Distractions 89

Chapter 9: Parental and Educator Involvement 92

9.1 How to Get Your Parents (or Another Adult) to *Actually* Listen to You 92

9.2 Creating a Supportive Environment at Home 96

9.3 How to Team Up with Your Teachers and Win at School 98

9.4 Teaming Up with Your Boss: How to Succeed at Work 101

9.5 Becoming a Boss at Adulting: Independence Made Easy (and Fun) 103

Chapter 10: Adulting: The Crash Course (With Extra Sass) 107

10.1 Ready for College? Let's Get Those Skills in Shape 107

10.2 Living Solo: It's a Whole Vibe 108

10.3 Workforce Adventures: Let's Do This 109

10.4 Work-Life Balance: The Ultimate Boss Move 110

10.5 Financial Independence: Budget Like a Boss and Manage Your Money 111

Conclusion **116**

Bonus Chapter : Navigating ADHD with Your Teen: A Guide for Parents **120**

Introduction: Embracing the Journey Together 120

11.1 Understanding ADHD: More Than Just Hyperactivity 120

11.2 Creating a Structured Environment: The Power of Routine 121

11.3 Fostering Effective Communication: Speak Their Language 123

11.4 Boosting Self-Esteem: Celebrate the Wins 124

11.5 Managing Emotional Regulation: Handling the Ups and Downs 125

11.6 Partnering with Educators: A Team Effort 127

11.7 Self-Care for Parents: You Matter Too 128

11.8 Types of Self-Care 131

References **136**

Introduction

Hey, You Amazing Human!

Let me kick this off with a little story. Picture me as a teenager, sitting at my desk, staring at what felt like an *avalanche* of homework. My brain was like a TV with 100 channels playing at once. I'd bounce from one idea to the next—thinking about math, then snacks, then *why is the sky blue*—and suddenly, *poof*, it was midnight, and I hadn't done squat. Sound familiar? Yeah, that's ADHD life for you. But here's the thing—you're not lazy, and you're definitely not alone. ADHD is like having a super-powered mind that just needs the right tools to shine. Lucky for you, those tools are exactly what this book is all about.

In my career, I've worked with tons of people who struggled with time management, meeting deadlines, and just staying on track. Sound like chaos? At first, sure. But once we started putting ADHD-friendly strategies into action—ones that fit their unique brains and needs—magic happened. Teams got organized, work started being fun (yes, FUN!), and success? Oh, we crushed it. That same transformation can happen for you.

This book is here to help you embrace your *neurodiverse awesomeness*. ADHD means your brain is wired a little differently (and honestly, how boring would it be if we were all the same?). We'll explore practical, simple hacks to tackle procrastination, get organized, and build independence. All without stress. Seriously.

Meet Your Guide

I'm Sabine, and I've spent years helping teens and young adults like you navigate ADHD and other neurodiverse superpowers. I get it—feeling like you're constantly running behind, no matter how hard you hustle, is exhausting. My goal? To help you discover ADHD-friendly strategies that don't just *work* but actually make life easier—and dare I say, even fun.

What's the Deal With ADHD?

Let's break it down. ADHD (Attention Deficit Hyperactivity Disorder) is a fancy way of saying your brain works differently when it comes to focus, organization, and impulse control. Then there's **Executive Functioning**, which is like your brain's project manager—it helps you manage time, make decisions, and stay organized. ADHD can make those things harder, but (big BUT here), that doesn't mean impossible. With a little practice and the right tools, you can level up these skills and tackle anything life throws your way.

A lot of teens and young adults with neurodiverse minds face similar challenges. Staying focused feels like climbing a mountain (without snacks). Impulsive decisions can land you in some sticky situations. And managing time? Sometimes it feels like time is managing *you*. Sound familiar? Then guess what—you're in the right place.

Why This Book Is Different

So, why should you keep reading? Because this book is all about *you*. It's not some boring manual that tells you to "try harder" (ugh). It's practical, no-BS, and packed with bite-sized strategies that won't stress you out. Each hack is designed to fit seamlessly into *your* life. No one-size-fits-all nonsense here.

We'll start by breaking down what Executive Functioning is and why it matters. Each chapter zooms in on areas where ADHD might trip you up—like time management, organization, or handling emotions—and gives you 10 easy hacks for each. It's like a choose-your-own-adventure guide for getting stuff done. By the end, you'll have a toolkit of habits that actually stick.

What's in It for You

More than just hacks and strategies, I want this book to feel like having a cheerleader in your corner (minus the pom-poms, but hey, they're optional). ADHD isn't just about challenges—it's about strengths, too. You've got unique talents, and with the right support, you can turn those quirks into *superpowers*. This book is all about progress, not perfection. We'll celebrate your wins—big or small—because every step forward matters.

Pro Tip Alert 🚨

Here's a hack to use *right now*. Whenever something in this book clicks—like, "Whoa, that's totally me!" or "I *have* to try this!"—bookmark the page immediately. ADHD brains are like race cars with no brakes, and trust me, in a few pages, your brain will have zoomed off to something else. Save yourself the "where was that amazing tip?" struggle later.

So, let's get started! Together, we'll tackle the ups, downs, and loop-de-loops of ADHD and neurodiversity. By the end, you'll have a roadmap to make life not just manageable, but *awesome.* Remember: you're not alone, you're not broken, and you've got what it takes to thrive. Let's do this! 🎉

Chapter 1

Understanding ADHD and Executive Functioning

Alright, Let's Get Real About ADHD

ADHD gets a bad rap sometimes, with people calling it a "disorder." Ugh, can we just pause on that for a second? Disorder literally means "DIS-ORDER," aka something different from the usual way things are organized. Guess what? You're not mainstream, and that's something to celebrate. 🎉

Having ADHD is like owning a brain that's customized. Sure, it can feel like the world is running on Windows while you're out here rocking a Mac—but different doesn't mean broken. It just means your brain works in its own unique way, and that comes with challenges *and* superpowers.

1.1 So, What Exactly Is ADHD?

You probably know ADHD stands for **Attention Deficit Hyperactivity Disorder**, but let's break it down. ADHD isn't just "I can't focus" or "I'm too hyper." It's a neurodevelopmental difference that impacts how your brain manages attention, organization, and impulses. Think of it like having a racecar engine in a world of minivans—it's fast, it's fun, but keeping it on the road? That's where things can get tricky.

ADHD Comes in Three Flavors:

1. **Inattentive Type** (often called ADD): You're the daydreamer, losing track of time and thoughts.

2. **Hyperactive-Impulsive Type**: You're the energizer bunny—fidgety, talkative, and ready to go 24/7.

3. **Combined Type**: A mix of both. Think of it as ADHD with extra toppings.

Knowing which type you lean towards helps you understand yourself better. And no, ADHD isn't an excuse for laziness or bad behavior—it's a legit brain difference.

Let's Bust Some ADHD Myths

1. **ADHD is just an excuse for being lazy.**

    Nope. ADHD isn't about effort; it's about how your brain regulates attention and impulses. Imagine trying to build a Lego set with the instructions constantly disappearing—it's not that you're lazy, it's just harder to get things done.

2. **Only boys have ADHD.**

    Wrong again. Girls often fly under the radar because their symptoms can look different. Instead of being hyper, they might daydream or quietly struggle with focus. ADHD doesn't care about gender—it's an equal opportunity brain quirk.

3. **It's caused by bad parenting.**

   Let's be clear: ADHD is about brain chemistry, not parenting. While supportive parents can help, they didn't *cause* ADHD.

The Science-y Stuff (It's Cool, I Promise)

Your brain has some VIP areas—like the prefrontal cortex and basal ganglia—that handle planning, focusing, and impulse control. In ADHD brains, these areas might be smaller or work differently. On top of that, the brain chemicals dopamine and norepinephrine don't always flow smoothly, which can make focusing or staying on task feel like trying to swim upstream.

1.2 Executive Functioning: Your Brain's Boss

Think of executive functioning as your brain's CEO. It's in charge of planning, organizing, and getting things done. Here's the breakdown:

- **Working Memory**: Your brain's sticky note for holding info, like remembering math steps or what you just read. ADHD? That sticky note keeps falling off.

- **Cognitive Flexibility**: Your ability to switch gears. Plans changed? ADHD might leave you stuck on the old plan.

- **Inhibitory Control**: Your brain's "pause button," helping you think before acting. With ADHD, that button can feel like it's jammed.

When executive functioning is glitchy, things like starting tasks, managing time, or staying organized can feel impossible. It's like your brain is running 25 tabs at once, and you can't find the music that's playing.

The Real-Life Struggles

Here's how ADHD might show up in your daily life:

- **Schoolwork**: Concentrating on homework feels like trying to catch a greased-up pig.
- **Social Stuff**: Impulses might make you blurt out things or struggle with friendships.
- **Emotions**: Feelings hit like a rollercoaster—big highs, deep lows, and no seatbelt.
- **Organization**: Your room, your backpack, your life... basically chaos central.

But don't freak out. Knowing *why* these challenges happen means you can tackle them head-on.

Why Your Brain Is Awesome (Yes, Really)

ADHD isn't all struggles. It comes with some serious perks:

- **Creativity**: Your brain thinks outside the box—heck, it probably doesn't even *see* the box.
- **Hyperfocus**: When you're into something, you go *all in*.
- **Problem-Solving**: You see solutions others miss, like a life hack machine.

The trick is learning how to harness these strengths while managing the tough stuff.

Tips for Thriving

Let's talk strategies. ADHD brains love *simple, clear* tools, so here's what can help:

- **Timers Are Your BFF**: Use alarms to break tasks into chunks. 15 minutes of focus, then a break.
- **Visual Reminders**: Sticky notes, color coding, apps—whatever keeps you on track.
- **Break It Down**: Big tasks = overwhelm. Break them into bite-sized steps.
- **Celebrate Wins**: Finished a task? High five yourself, grab a snack, and do a victory dance.

Final Thoughts

ADHD is just one part of who you are—it doesn't define you. With the right hacks and support, you can turn challenges into superpowers and live a life that's uniquely *you*. So buckle up, ADHD brain—it's gonna be an epic ride. Let's get started! 🚀

ADHD Challenges: Keeping It Real, and How to Crush It

Let's be real: life with ADHD isn't a walk in the park—it's more like trying to herd a group of caffeinated squirrels. But hey, that doesn't mean you can't handle it! Let's break down some of the trickiest hurdles ADHD can throw at you and how to leap over them with style. Buckle up—this is gonna be fun (and useful).

🎓 School Stuff: Where's My Homework?

Being a student with ADHD can feel like playing dodgeball blindfolded. Everyone else seems to be catching and throwing, and you're just trying not to get hit. Sound familiar? Here's why:

- **Focus Fail:** Sitting in class, trying to listen, but your brain's like, "Ooh, tacos for lunch!" It's not that you don't care; your brain's just wired to wander.

- **Backpack Black Hole:** Is your bag an abyss where math assignments go to die? Keeping track of papers and supplies feels like a full-time job.

- **Procrastination Olympics:** "I'll do it later" turns into "OMG, it's due tomorrow!" You convince yourself you're great under pressure (you're not, but we love your optimism).

👉 **Hack It!** Use color-coded folders, apps like Notion or Google Keep, and set alarms to remind you about assignments. Bonus points for getting a friend or parent to be your "accountability buddy."

🤝 Social Shenanigans: Wait, Was That Awkward?

ADHD can make social stuff feel like playing a game you don't know the rules to. Here's the deal:

- **Blurt Alert:** You're mid-conversation, and BOOM—you interrupt with your brilliant idea. You're not rude; you're just...excited.

- **Missing the Memo:** Body language and tone? What's that? Misreading cues can make things weird.

- **Friendship Juggle:** Forgetting plans or zoning out during hangouts can leave pals feeling hurt. Maintaining friendships? It's tricky.

👉 **Hack It!** Practice active listening—think of it like playing catch: they talk, you "catch," then respond. Use sticky notes or phone reminders for plans so you're always on point.

🌈 Mood Swings and Feels: The Emotional Rollercoaster

With ADHD, emotions can go from zero to 💯 in seconds. One minute you're happy; the next, you're Hulk-smashing your way through frustration.

- **Mood Mayhem:** That "top of the world" feeling? Awesome. But the lows? Not so much.
- **Rage Quit Moments:** Little things feel HUGE, like your sibling breathing too loud.
- **Emotional Hangover:** Big feelings can leave you drained and unsure how to bounce back.

👉 **Hack It!** Take deep breaths, journal, or try mindfulness apps like Calm or Headspace. Learning to name your emotions (e.g., "I'm frustrated") can actually help you tame them.

🧠 Executive Dysfunction: The Ultimate Brain Boss Fight

ADHD messes with your Executive Functioning—the brain's control center. Without it, life's like trying to drive a car with no brakes and a sticky accelerator.

- **Time Blindness:** You sit down to study at 7 PM, blink, and suddenly it's 9. How?!

- **Task Pile-Up:** Your to-do list feels like Mount Everest, and starting anything is like climbing it barefoot.
- **Clutter Chaos:** Your room? Disaster zone. Keeping things tidy feels impossible.

👉 **Hack It!** Break tasks into bite-sized pieces (e.g., "Write intro paragraph" instead of "Finish essay"). Use timers—try the Pomodoro Technique (25 minutes work, 5 minutes break). And keep your workspace simple—less clutter, less stress.

😨 Stress, Anxiety, and Extra Baggage

ADHD often comes with *bonus* challenges like anxiety, depression, or learning differences. Thanks, brain.

- **Anxiety Overload:** Overthinking EVERYTHING—did I say the wrong thing? Will I fail this test? Ugh.
- **Depression Slumps:** ADHD can drain your energy and motivation, making you feel stuck.
- **Learning Curve:** If you have a learning disability, school might feel like running uphill in flip-flops.

👉 **Hack It!** Therapy can be a game-changer. Don't be afraid to talk to a counselor or therapist—they're like personal trainers for your brain. Also, celebrate *every* win, no matter how small. Got out of bed? High five.

🛠 Building Better Habits (Yes, It's Possible!)

Let's talk routines. No, they're not boring—they're like cheat codes for ADHD.

- **Morning Power-Up:** Wake up, eat, check your planner—same order, every day. Boom, you're ready to rock.

- **Evening Wind-Down:** Pack your bag, lay out clothes, set alarms. Future you will be grateful.
- **Money Moves:** Keep track of spending so you don't blow your paycheck on snacks and impulse buys.

Why You're Actually a Superhero

Here's the tea: ADHD isn't just about challenges—it comes with some epic strengths.

- **Creative Genius:** Your brain connects dots others don't even see.
- **Hyperfocus Power:** When you're into something, you *crush it.*
- **Big Picture Thinker:** While others sweat the small stuff, you dream big.

You've Got This

Life with ADHD is like playing life on "Hard Mode." But with the right hacks and support, you can absolutely level up. This book is here to give you the tools, the tips, and the encouragement to be your best, most badass self.

You're not broken; you're just built differently. And that? That's a superpower. Now, go show the world what you've got!

1.3 Setting the Stage for Success: What's in It for You?

Hey there! So, what's the deal with this book, and why should you care? Well, buckle up, because this is not your average boring self-help manual. We're diving into the nitty-gritty of ADHD struggles and coming out the other side with tools, tips, and hacks that actually work. Think of this as your ADHD survival kit—designed to help you crush life, one challenge at a time.

Here's the game plan: each chapter is like a mini-mission, zooming in on a specific problem and giving you battle-tested strategies to tackle it. No fluff, no judgment—just real talk and practical solutions. First up: **time management**, because let's face it, time is slippery when you've got ADHD. We'll explore tricks like the Pomodoro Technique (a fancy way of saying "work hard, take breaks") and time blocking, which is basically your day's cheat code.

But that's just the start. Got procrastination problems? Who doesn't? We'll smash that habit with hacks like the **Two-Minute Rule** (if it's quick, just do it already) and instant reward systems that make getting stuff done almost... fun. Almost.

And let's not forget **organization skills**—the holy grail for ADHD brains. Say goodbye to the black hole of doom that is your backpack. We'll teach you how to declutter, create visual cues, and use digital tools so your stuff doesn't go MIA every five minutes.

This isn't about boring lectures or impossible goals. It's about small, manageable wins—like finding your homework *before* class starts or not losing your keys for the fifth time this week. You'll also hear success stories from other teens who've been in the trenches. Spoiler: they made it out, and so can you.

Most importantly, this is a **judgment-free zone**. ADHD isn't about laziness or carelessness; it's about having a brain that dances to its own beat. This book is here to help you embrace that rhythm and make it work for you. So, no, you're not aiming for perfection—we're aiming for progress, and that's something worth celebrating.

Chapter 2

Time Management Techniques for ADHD Legends

Okay, so you know the feeling: you sit down to crush some homework, and five YouTube cat videos later, you're like, *Wait, what was I doing?* Time is slippery—especially with ADHD. But don't stress, because we've got tools to wrestle it back under control. Ready? Let's roll.

2.1 The Pomodoro Technique: Your New Secret Weapon

First up, meet the **Pomodoro Technique**, the ultimate ADHD-friendly hack. Why the fancy name? Blame the Italian inventor who used a tomato-shaped timer. (Pomodoro means tomato. Cute, right?) Here's the deal:

1. Pick a task—any task. Maybe it's math homework, cleaning your room, or finally reading that assigned chapter.

2. Set a timer for 25 minutes. That's one "Pomodoro."

3. Work like a beast until the timer dings. Then take a 5-minute break. Scroll Instagram, do some stretches—whatever recharges your brain.

4. After four Pomodoros, reward yourself with a longer break. (Snack time, anyone?)

Why does this work? It's ADHD kryptonite. The timer gives you urgency, the short bursts keep you focused, and the breaks stop burnout. Plus, it feels *so* satisfying to rack up completed Pomodoros. You're basically a productivity ninja now.

> **Pro Tip:** *There are apps for this—TomatoTimer, Forest, or Focus Booster. No excuses.*

2.2 Time Blocking: The Art of Owning Your Day

Imagine this: you wake up, check your schedule, and bam—you know exactly what's happening today. No guesswork, no chaos, no "Wait, was that due *today*?" That's time blocking, and it's about to be your new best friend.

Here's how it works:

1. **Write it down.** Make a list of everything you need to do—homework, sports, Netflix binges (yes, relaxation counts).

2. **Block it out.** Assign each task a specific chunk of time on your calendar.

3. **Stick to the plan**—mostly. Life happens, so leave some wiggle room for surprises.

Here's an example:

- **7:00 AM–8:00 AM:** Morning routine (aka pretending to be awake).
- **8:30 AM–12:00 PM:** School/college/work.
- **12:00 PM–1:00 PM:** Lunch. Maybe squeeze in some TikTok.
- **3:00 PM–5:00 PM:** Extracurriculars—sports, band practice, hanging with friends.
- **6:00 PM–8:00 PM:** Study time. Yes, you have to.
- **8:30 PM–10:00 PM:** Chill. You earned it.

Why is this magic? Because when you've got a plan, there's less time for *What do I do next?* panic. You're in control, and your ADHD brain LOVES structure—it just doesn't know it yet.

Hacks for Staying on Track

- **Keep it real.** Don't block every second; leave room to breathe.
- **Use alarms.** Seriously, your phone is your ally. Set reminders so you don't miss stuff.
- **Adjust as needed.** If something takes longer than planned, it's okay. Just shuffle the blocks around.

Time management isn't about becoming a robot. It's about finding a flow that works for you—whether that's working in Pomodoro sprints or carving out blocks of time for your priorities. It's your day. You're the boss. Go get it!

2.3 Time Management Superpowers: Digital Tools Edition

Managing time with ADHD can feel like playing dodgeball with your to-do list—it's everywhere, and it keeps coming. But guess what? Your phone isn't just for TikTok binges; it can actually *help* you crush your schedule. Digital tools are like the sidekick you didn't know you needed. They're smart, fast, and don't judge you for missing yesterday's alarm. Let's dive into how apps and alarms can level up your time management game.

App-tastic Time Management

- **Google Calendar**: Think of it as your life's colorful, organized playbook. Assign tasks to specific times (like "Math Homework, 4–5 PM"), color-code them (blue for school, red for fun, green for stuff like walking the dog), and set alarms so you don't "accidentally" scroll Instagram for three hours instead.

- **Todoist**: It's like your brain, but with checkboxes. Break tasks into steps, slap on some deadlines, and rank them by importance. It's perfect for tracking that English paper, science project, *and* remembering to feed your pet cactus.

- **Forest**: Procrastination killer + tree hugger. You set a timer, and while you work, a virtual tree grows. But if you bail to check memes, your tree dies. No one wants to be a tree killer—stay on task and build a whole digital forest.

How to Maximize Your Digital Sidekicks

1. **Start Small**: Plug in tomorrow's tasks, like your math homework, soccer practice, and post-practice snack break (important).
2. **Set Alarms**: Layer reminders—one 30 minutes before ("Get your head in the game!") and another when it's time to dive in ("Do it. Now.").
3. **Sync It Up**: Link your calendar with your school's schedule or your extracurriculars. It's like assembling the Avengers, but for your time.
4. **Customize**: Adjust how these tools talk to you. Prefer soft pings? Cool. Need loud buzzers because you zone out? Go for it.

Digital tools aren't magic wands, but they're close. They keep you on track, make life feel less overwhelming, and are way more reliable than your brain at remembering stuff.

2.4 Daily Routines: The Chill Way to Stay on Track

Think "routine" sounds boring? Plot twist: routines are actually your secret weapon against chaos. They're like a script for your day, so you can focus on *doing* instead of figuring out what's next.

Building the Best Routine for You

1. **List Your Non-Negotiables**: Start with the basics—waking up, eating, school, study time, Netflix marathons (ok, maybe limit those).
2. **Block Time**: Assign specific time slots for everything. Need 30 minutes for your skincare routine? Lock it in.

Homework? Schedule it and sprinkle in breaks to avoid brain fog.

3. **Flex, Don't Stress**: Life happens. If something runs long (like arguing with your sibling about who gets the last cookie), just adjust. Routines aren't the boss of you; they're your guide.

Morning and Evening Power Moves

- **Morning Routine**: Rise at the same time daily (yes, weekends count). A quick shower, breakfast, and checking your calendar can put you in beast mode for the day.

- **Evening Routine**: Wind down with calming activities—no, doomscrolling doesn't count. Pick out your outfit, pack your bag, and lay out tomorrow's plan so future you can breathe easy.

Routines take the stress out of the unknown. They're your daily armor against chaos, and once you nail them, they'll feel like second nature.

2.5 Quick Wins: Treat Yo' Self!

Who doesn't love a reward? Quick wins are like giving yourself a high-five for adulting. And let's be real—sometimes we all need a little bribe to get stuff done. ADHD brains thrive on instant gratification, so these little rewards are game-changers.

Set Up Your Reward System

1. **Pick the Task**: Got homework? Cleaning your disaster zone of a room? Choose your challenge.

2. **Dangle the Carrot**: Rewards can be tiny but mighty. Think "15 minutes of gaming," "snack time," or "scrolling TikTok guilt-free."

3. **Track Progress**: Use a chart or app to check off tasks and unlock your reward. Watching the boxes fill up is oddly satisfying.

Reward Examples to Get You Started

- **Math Homework**: Finish a problem set, earn a YouTube break. Laugh at cat videos guilt-free.

- **Biology Notes**: Knock out 25 minutes of studying and grab a handful of candy.

- **Clean-Up Duty**: Tidy your desk, win 20 minutes of gaming. Bonus points if you find that pencil you lost three weeks ago.

Rewards make even the lamest tasks doable because there's something fun waiting at the finish line. Start small, keep it personal, and watch as you become the ultimate task-slaying machine.

With digital tools, a solid routine, and fun rewards, time management doesn't have to suck. You've got the hacks—now go crush your day! Also, my reward for writing this? Extra guac on my taco.

Chapter 3

Busting Procrastination: Getting Started

Ever found yourself staring at a blank screen, knowing you need to start that essay, but somehow, you just can't? Maybe you decide to clean your room instead, or get lost in a YouTube rabbit hole. Procrastination is a common challenge. It feels like a giant wall between you and getting things done. But what if I told you there's a way to break down that wall, one small brick at a time? Enter the Two-Minute Rule, a simple yet powerful hack to help you get started.

3.1 The Two-Minute Rule: Beat Procrastination by Starting Small

Procrastination—sound familiar? Instead of diving into tasks, you scroll your phone or play a game. It's normal! The trick is to break tasks into smaller steps and reward yourself along the way. That's where the **Two-Minute Rule** comes in.

The rule is simple: if something takes two minutes or less, do it now. It helps you overcome that "where do I start?" feeling and gets you moving, just like stretching before a workout preps athletes.

How It Works

Here's an example from my day:

Tasks:

- Contact the supervisor.
- Email team leaders new rules.
- Talk to the team about policies.
- Book a GP appointment (ugh, my throat hurts).
- Call my parents (it's been a while).
- Write a long report (hours of work 😖).

Cue overwhelm... TikTok break? NOPE.

Stop. Two-Minute Rule time:

1. Quick email to the supervisor (30 seconds). ☑
2. Longer email to team leaders (1 minute). ☑
3. Schedule a meeting with the team (30 seconds). ☑
4. Call GP—on hold for 3 minutes, but DONE. ☑
5. Add "call parents" to calendar with a reminder (30 seconds). ☑

Boom—five tasks done in under 12 minutes! I feel amazing, reward myself with chocolate chip cookies, a quick walk, and smiles for my coworkers. With just one big task left, I'm ready to crush it!

Why It Works

Small wins build momentum. Tidy your desk, send that email, or write one sentence of an essay. Starting small makes big tasks feel doable, and confidence grows with every step. Give it a try—you'll love how productive (and awesome) you feel!

Here Are Some Examples:

- Messy Desk: If your desk is a disaster and you can't find anything, don't stress about a big clean-up. Just take two minutes to put away some books or organize your pens. Before you know it, your desk will look much better, and you'll feel ready to tackle more!

- Writing an Essay: Starting an essay can be scary, but writing just the first sentence quickly and easily. Once you've done that, it'll feel less daunting to keep writing.

- Sending an Email: If you've been meaning to ask your teacher a question but keep putting it off, use two minutes to type and send that email. It's done before you know it, and you'll clear that mental block!

Why It's so Awesome :

The Two-Minute Rule is super flexible! You can use it for pretty much any task, big or small. It's all about creating a habit of action. The more you use this rule, the easier it gets to tackle tasks without procrastinating.

So, the next time you feel stuck, remember the Two-Minute Rule! Start small, and let those little actions lead to bigger wins. You'll be amazed at how much you can accomplish, two minutes at a time! You've got this! 🚀

3.2 Instant Gratification Techniques: Small Rewards for Big Wins

Boost Your Motivation with Instant Rewards!

Ever feel like starting a task is just *ugh* too boring or pointless? You're not alone! That's where instant rewards come to the rescue. The concept is simple: treat yourself to something small and fun every time you finish a task. It's like training your brain to think, *"Work = Yay!"*

For teens (especially with ADHD) and honestly everyone else, this trick is a total game-changer. Immediate rewards make it easier to stay focused and power through. With a reward waiting at the finish line, even boring chores can feel like leveling up in a game.

How to Set Up Your Reward System

1. **List Your Tasks:** Homework, cleaning, or even replying to texts you've been avoiding.

2. **Pick Rewards:** Choose little treats that make you happy—a quick game, a snack, or 5 minutes of TikTok. Keep them simple but fun!

3. **Track Your Progress:** Use a checklist or journal to see how much you're crushing it.

Fun Reward Ideas

- **Math Problems:** Finished a tough set? Watch a funny video or scroll Instagram for 5 minutes.

- **Studying:** After 30 minutes, grab your favorite snack. Brain fuel!

- **Cleaning:** Done organizing? Reward yourself with 10 minutes of gaming.

Stay Consistent and Make It Yours

The key is sticking with it! Reward yourself for every task, no matter how small, to keep building momentum. Everyone's different, so test out rewards to find what really excites you—snacks, games, or even a quick nap.

Instant rewards turn "blah" chores into exciting challenges. With every small win, you'll feel more motivated and ready to tackle the next thing on your list. You've got this—start rewarding yourself and see how fun productivity can be! 🎉

3.3 Tackling the Worst First: How to Get the Hard Stuff Out of the Way

Unlock Your Motivation with Instant Rewards!

Ever feel like starting a task is just *too much effort*? You're not alone! That's where instant rewards save the day. The idea's simple: treat yourself to small rewards for finishing tasks. These little boosts make work feel fun, not boring—how cool is that?

For teens with ADHD (and honestly, everyone), this can be a game-changer. Immediate rewards keep you focused and make sticking to tasks easier. Knowing there's a treat waiting turns boring chores into fun challenges, like leveling up in a game!

How to Set Up Your Reward System

1. **Make a Task List:** Homework, cleaning, or replying to texts—whatever needs doing.
2. **Choose Rewards:** Snacks, 5 minutes of TikTok, or a quick game—pick what makes you happy!
3. **Track Progress:** Use a checklist or journal to see your wins pile up.

Fun Reward Ideas

- **Math Problems:** Finished a set? Watch a funny video or scroll Instagram for 5 minutes.
- **Studying:** After 30 minutes, grab your favorite snack. Brain fuel!
- **Cleaning:** Done organizing? Reward yourself with 10 minutes of gaming.

Stay Consistent and Make It Yours

Reward every win, no matter how small, and stick with it. Try different rewards—what works for one person might not work for you.

Instant rewards turn boring tasks into exciting wins. Each little boost builds momentum and keeps you going. Start rewarding yourself today—you've got this! 🎉

3.4 The Power of Music: Using Playlists to Boost Focus

How Music Can Help You Crush Your Study Sessions

Let's be real: studying in silence can feel like watching paint dry. But crank up the right tunes, and suddenly, that history essay isn't so bad. Remember when your parents would yell, *"Turn that noise down! You can't possibly study with all that racket!"* Well, joke's on them because music might actually be your secret weapon for getting stuff done. (Also, hello, noise-cancelling headphones—game-changer.)

Ready to learn how music can turbocharge your focus? Let's dive in and crank up the volume on your study sessions!

Why Music Makes You Smarter (Kind Of)

Music isn't just background noise—it's a focus hack that works for your brain in surprising ways. Here's how:

- **Blocks Distractions**: Whether it's your little brother screaming about his Fortnite win or that weird bird outside your window, music helps drown out the noise. It's like creating a bubble of "leave me alone" vibes.

- **Sets the Mood**: Chill tracks can calm you down, while upbeat jams can energize you for those late-night cram sessions.

- **Activates Flow State**: The right music can nudge you into a rhythm where everything clicks, and time flies (well, mostly).

The Playlist of Power: Different Genres for Different Vibes

Not all music is created equal for studying. Picking the right tunes depends on what you're doing and how easily you get distracted.

1. Instrumental Magic: Lyrics Are So Overrated

Ever tried to write an essay while listening to your favorite pop songs? Yeah, good luck typing coherent sentences when your brain is busy belting out lyrics. Instrumental tracks keep your brain focused without the lyrical drama.

- **Classical Music**: Beethoven, Bach, or some lo-fi piano vibes—it's basically a brain massage.

- **Soundtracks**: Ever notice how epic movie scores make you feel invincible? Try Hans Zimmer or the "Stranger Things" theme. You'll feel like a productivity superhero.

2. Lo-Fi Beats: The Chill Champion

Lo-fi music has exploded recently (you've seen those endless "lo-fi girl studying" YouTube streams). Its mellow beats and lack of lyrics make it perfect for zoning in without zoning out. Bonus: the vibe is immaculate.

3. Upbeat Bangers: When You Need Energy

For tasks that need creativity (or keeping your eyes open), some pump-up jams can help. Think EDM, K-pop, or even '80s rock anthems. The energy will keep you moving, but stick to instrumental versions if lyrics mess with your focus.

4. White Noise & Ambient Sounds: The Zen Zone

Not a fan of "music" music? White noise and ambient sounds can be just as effective. Apps like **Rainy Mood** or **Noisli** play calming soundscapes like ocean waves, crackling fire, or even coffee shop chatter (without the actual people).

The Role of Contemporary Music as White Noise

Here's where it gets cool: some of today's popular genres double as white noise. Think low-energy electronic music or ambient pop—it's music that blends into the background while still giving you a rhythm to work to.

Artists to Check Out

- **Tycho**: Dreamy, instrumental vibes perfect for staying in the zone.
- **ODESZA**: A mix of chill electronic and subtle beats—great for focus with a touch of groove.
- **Billie Eilish's Slower Tracks**: Songs like *"when the party's over"* can create a calm, focused atmosphere.

- **Joji's Instrumentals**: Minimal lyrics, maximum vibe.
- **Bonobo**: Atmospheric electronic music that's like a sonic hug for your brain.

Pro tip: Search for "study playlists" on Spotify or YouTube, and you'll find a treasure trove of curated tunes designed to help you lock in.

Building Your Ultimate Study Soundtrack

Not all study sessions are the same, so your playlist shouldn't be, either. Here's how to craft the perfect mix for every vibe:

Step 1: Start Chill

Ease into your study mode with calm, low-energy tracks. Lo-fi beats or ambient tracks are your warm-up.

Step 2: Ramp It Up

When you hit your groove, switch to more upbeat, instrumental tracks to keep the momentum going.

Step 3: Cool It Down

Wrap up with something soothing—this helps you wind down and process what you've learned.

Study Scenarios and Music Matches

1. Homework Grind

- **Music Match**: Lo-fi beats, soft indie instrumentals, or ambient electronic.
- **Why**: Keeps you calm and focused without making you feel sleepy.

2. Exam Prep Mode

- **Music Match**: Classical piano or white noise.
- **Why**: Zero distractions—just pure focus fuel.

3. Creative Writing or Art Projects

- **Music Match**: Chillwave, dreamy pop, or acoustic tracks.
- **Why**: Boosts creativity without overwhelming your brain.

4. Last-Minute Cramming

- **Music Match**: Upbeat instrumentals or fast-paced electronic.
- **Why**: Keeps you alert and energized when the clock's ticking.

Quick Tips for Using Music Effectively 🎉

1. **Headphones Are Key**: Invest in noise-cancelling headphones—they're worth every penny.
2. **Keep It Consistent**: Use the same playlist for studying so your brain associates it with focus time.
3. **Volume Matters**: Keep it low enough to avoid drowning out your thoughts.
4. **Experiment**: Not every track works for everyone. Try different genres and see what clicks.

When Music Doesn't Work (Yes, It Happens)

Not feeling it? That's okay. Some people find even the chillest tunes distracting. If music isn't your jam, stick to ambient sounds or total silence (if you can find it).

Interactive Playlist Challenge: Make It Fun

Get your friends involved! Create a collaborative playlist where everyone adds their favorite focus tracks. You might discover some gems you never thought to try.

Music and the Science of ADHD Brains

If you've got ADHD, you already know that staying focused can be like herding cats. Music can be a secret weapon because:

- **It Regulates Your Mood**: Chill tracks can calm you down, while upbeat ones can energize you.

- **It Provides Structure**: Rhythmic music acts like a metronome for your brain, helping you stay on task.

Wrap It Up: Study Smarter with Music

Music isn't just a vibe—it's a tool. The right playlist can turn even the most boring study session into something you almost (dare we say it?) enjoy.

So, grab your headphones, build your ultimate study playlist, and crank up the focus. You've got this. And if anyone tells you to turn it down? Smile and say, *"I'm working on my future."* 🎵 ✨

Chapter 4

How to Get Your Life Together Without Losing Your Mind 🎉

Let's face it: adulting is hard. One minute, you're thriving, and the next, your room looks like a tornado ripped through it, your homework's missing, and your mom's yelling about the state of your backpack. Sound familiar? Don't worry—you're not alone. Organization might not sound glamorous, but it's your secret weapon for crushing school, life, and everything in between.

And hey, if you're someone who thrives on chaos (*looking at you, "floor-closet" enthusiasts*), this guide is for you too. Let's make organization fun, functional, and maybe even a little bit addictive. Ready? Let's roll.

4.1 Accountability Buddies: Your New Sidekick

Ever wish you had someone to remind you to *actually* do your homework, clean your room, or tackle that mountain of laundry? Meet the accountability buddy—part hype-person, part life coach, and 100% there to make sure you don't procrastinate yourself into oblivion.

Why You Need a Buddy

- **They Keep You Honest**: Skipping your to-do list is way harder when someone's going to ask, *"Did you finish that project yet?"*
- **It's Less Lonely**: Misery loves company—why suffer alone when you can drag a friend into the chaos?
- **They're Your Cheerleader**: They'll celebrate your wins and give you a pep talk when you're struggling.

How to Pick the Right Buddy

Choose someone you trust, who's reliable (aka won't flake), and who's cool with checking in regularly. Bonus points if they're also trying to stay on top of their stuff—it's teamwork at its finest.

How to Buddy Up Like a Pro

- **Set Clear Goals**: Whether it's studying, organizing, or just surviving the week, decide what you're working on together.
- **Check-In Regularly**: Pick a time to chat—daily, weekly, whatever works. Pro tip: Turn it into a virtual hangout with snacks.
- **Make It Fun**: Share playlists, use funny memes to motivate each other, or turn tasks into mini-competitions.

4.2 Decluttering: Because Your Room Deserves Better

Raise your hand if your "cleaning strategy" involves shoving everything under the bed and hoping no one looks. No judgment, but let's aim higher, shall we? A tidy space equals a tidy mind—or at least fewer things to trip over.

Why Decluttering Matters

Mess equals stress. A chaotic environment makes it harder to focus and can secretly drain your energy. Plus, let's be real: finding your math homework buried under three weeks' worth of laundry is *not* a vibe.

How to Declutter Without Crying

1. **Start Small**: Don't try to tackle your entire room in one go—that's how people end up sobbing into their old yearbooks. Pick a single area, like your desk or closet.

2. **Sort Like a Pro**:
    - **Keep**: Things you actually use.
    - **Donate**: Stuff in good condition you don't need.
    - **Trash**: The gum wrappers and dried-up pens you've been hoarding.

3. **Set a Timer**: Spend 15-20 minutes decluttering—it's way less intimidating than an all-day marathon.

4. **One In, One Out**: Got new sneakers? Say goodbye to the pair with holes that scream "middle school."

Fun Decluttering Challenges

- **Desk Detox**: Clear off papers, corral random chargers, and ditch the sticky notes that say, "Don't forget!" (but forgot what).

- **Backpack Purge**: Toss old assignments, snack wrappers, and whatever that weird smell is (seriously, check your gym shoes).

- **Closet Glow-Up**: Say goodbye to clothes that don't fit or spark joy—and hello to a wardrobe you can actually navigate.

4.3 The Art of Getting Organized: Make It Fun

Being organized isn't just about putting things in neat little piles—it's about creating systems that make life easier. The trick? Make it *your own*.

Step 1: Plan Like a Boss

- **Daily To-Do Lists**: Write down everything you need to do, even the small stuff. Crossing off "brush teeth" feels ridiculously satisfying.

- **Weekly Goals**: Big picture vibes—what do you want to accomplish this week?

- **Digital or Paper?**: Apps like Google Keep or Notion are great for tech lovers, but nothing beats a cute planner with stickers if you're old-school.

Step 2: Color-Code Everything

Highlighters aren't just for studying. Use colors to organize your planner, folders, or even your room (blue for schoolwork, green for fun, red for "DO THIS NOW OR ELSE").

Step 3: Create Stations

Think of your space like a theme park—every area should have a purpose.

- **Study Station**: Desk, chair, good lighting, and zero distractions.
- **Chill Zone**: Comfy spot for reading, journaling, or scrolling TikTok guilt-free.
- **Drop Zone**: A dedicated place for keys, backpacks, and random stuff so it doesn't explode across your room.

Step 4: Make It Visual

If you can see it, you're more likely to do it. Try:

- **Vision Boards**: Cut out pics of goals, quotes, or just cool aesthetics and pin them up.
- **Checklists**: There's nothing more satisfying than crossing things off.
- **Sticky Notes**: Scatter them everywhere as reminders—on your mirror, desk, or even your fridge.

4.5 Procrastination-Proofing Your Life ⏰

Raise your hand if you've ever said, *"I'll do it later,"* and then suddenly it's 2 a.m., and you're crying over an unfinished essay. Procrastination is the enemy, but don't worry—there are ways to fight back.

☞ **Hack #1: The Two-Minute Rule**

If something takes less than two minutes (like sending an email or putting away your shoes), do it now. It's faster than the time you'll waste thinking about doing it later.

☞ **Hack #2: Reward Yourself**

Turn boring tasks into games. Fold your laundry? Treat yourself to a Netflix episode. Finish a paper? Break out the snacks.

☞ **Hack #3: Break It Down**

Big projects are overwhelming, so slice them into bite-sized tasks. Writing an essay? Start with the title, then tackle the intro, and so on.

☞ **Hack #4: Set Alarms for EVERYTHING**

Seriously. Use your phone to remind you when to start studying, clean your room, or even take a snack break (important).

4.5 Your Game Plan for Staying Organized

Life's messy, and that's okay. The key is building habits that keep you on track—even when chaos strikes.

☞ **Morning Routines**

Start your day with a quick tidy-up, a glance at your planner, and maybe some pump-up music to set the mood.

☞ **Evening Wind-Downs**

Spend 10 minutes organizing your stuff for tomorrow. Future you will thank you.

☞ **Regular Check-Ins**

Take 15 minutes every week to review your goals, update your planner, and shuffle your to-do list. It's like a life reboot.

Final Thoughts: You've Got This! 🚀

Getting organized doesn't have to be boring or stressful. With a few hacks, some creativity, and maybe an accountability buddy, you can take control of your space, your time, and your brain.

And hey, if all else fails, just remember: one step at a time. Even the most organized people didn't figure it out overnight. You're doing great—and your glow-up is just getting started. ✨

Chapter 5

Emotional Regulation and Mindfulness

Feeling Stressed in Class? Here's How to Chill (ADHD Edition)

Ever been in class, and BAM—your heart's racing, your brain's in overdrive, and your palms are sweating like crazy? It's like the room's closing in, and all you wanna do is *get out*. If you've got ADHD, you've probably been there. Good news: you can totally hit pause on that overwhelm with one simple tool—deep breathing. Yep, it's not just for yoga moms; it's for you too.

5.1 Breathing Hacks: Calm Down Anytime, Anywhere

Deep breathing is like a secret weapon for anxiety and stress. Slow, deep breaths send a "chill out" signal to your brain, which helps your heart stop racing and your mind slow down. It's like a hard reset for your brain. Bonus? It even trains your body to handle stress better in the future.

Here are three super-easy breathing tricks to keep in your back pocket:

1. **4-7-8 Breathing**
   - Inhale through your nose for 4 seconds.
   - Hold it for 7 seconds.
   - Exhale through your mouth for 8 seconds.
   - Repeat a few times and feel the calm kick in.

2. **Box Breathing** (a.k.a. "drawing a square with your breath")
   - Inhale for 4 seconds.
   - Hold it for 4 seconds.
   - Exhale for 4 seconds.
   - Hold again for 4 seconds.
   - Rinse and repeat!

3. **Belly Breathing**
   - Put one hand on your belly and the other on your chest.
   - Take a deep breath, letting your belly (not your chest) puff out.
   - Exhale slowly, feeling your belly sink back in.

The next time you're stressed before a test or overwhelmed at school, try one of these. They're quick, easy, and make a *huge* difference.

5.2 Meditation for ADHD Minds: Chill Without the Effort

Got a brain that runs a million miles an hour? Meditation might sound impossible, but hear me out—it's actually perfect for you. Think of it like hitting the "pause" button on life. It's quick, easy, and helps you focus better and freak out less.

How to Start? Guided Meditation FTW.

Download an app (like Headspace or Calm) or hit up YouTube. A soothing voice will guide you through the whole thing—no awkward silence, no guesswork. Just pop in your headphones, find a comfy spot, and let the magic happen.

5.3 Journaling: Vent, Reflect, and Reset

Sometimes, the best way to deal with chaos in your brain is to spill it out onto paper. Journaling is like talking to your BFF—except this BFF *never* judges.

Here's how:

- **Free Write:** Let your thoughts pour out—no grammar, no structure, just go.
- **Prompts:** Answer questions like "What's stressing me out today?" or "What made me happy?"
- **Gratitude Lists:** Write 3 things you're grateful for. Even if it's just "pizza," "sunshine," or "my dog."

Do it every day, or just when life gets overwhelming. It's a simple habit that can help you understand yourself better and feel more in control.

5.4 The Stress Bucket: Empty It Before It Overflows

Picture your stress like a bucket filling with water. School, friends, family drama—each adds a little more water. When it overflows? Hello, meltdown.

How to Keep Your Bucket in Check:

- **Exercise:** Run, dance, or shoot some hoops—movement helps drain that stress.
- **Hobbies:** Lose yourself in something fun, like drawing, gaming, or baking.
- **Breaks:** Schedule short pauses in your day to breathe, stretch, or chill.

5.5 Resilience: Your Superpower for Bouncing Back

Life's messy, and setbacks happen. Building resilience means you can bounce back like a pro.

- **Growth Mindset:** See challenges as chances to grow, not reasons to quit.
- **Support Network:** Lean on friends, family, or a trusted teacher.
- **Self-Compassion:** Messed up? It's fine. Treat yourself with the kindness you'd give your best friend.

Resilience isn't about being perfect; it's about keeping it together when life gets tough. With practice, you'll feel stronger, more confident, and ready to handle whatever comes your way.

Take it one step at a time. You've got this!

Chapter 6

Boosting Self-Esteem and Building Confidence

Imagine you're scrolling through social media and see a post from a friend who just aced their math test, got promoted in their part-time job, and still had time to hang out with friends.

Meanwhile, you're struggling to finish your homework and feel like you're always playing catch-up. It's easy to feel down on yourself, especially when you have ADHD.

But here's the thing: building self-esteem and confidence isn't about comparing yourself to others. It's about recognizing your own unique strengths and celebrating your progress. Let's dive into how you can do that.

6.1 Self-Reflection Exercises: Recognizing Your Strengths

Let's Talk Self-Reflection: Your Secret Confidence Booster!

Okay, so self-reflection might sound super deep, like something you'd do while staring out at the ocean, but hear me out—it's actually way simpler (and cooler) than it sounds. Think of it as a mini reality check with yourself to figure out what makes you *you*.

It's like creating a cheat sheet for your talents, strengths, and even areas you want to level up in. And the best part? It's all about celebrating what makes you awesome.

For anyone with ADHD, self-reflection is a total game-changer. You're probably used to hearing about the stuff that's tough—like staying on task or managing time—but self-reflection flips that script *hard*. It's about zooming in on the good stuff, the things you rock at naturally. When you start focusing on your wins, you'll build self-awareness and confidence. You'll stop defining yourself by challenges and start seeing the incredible things you bring to the table.

So, How Do You Start?

Here's the good news: self-reflection doesn't have to be a huge project. It can be quick, fun, and super creative. Let's dive into some easy ways to make it work for you:

1. Daily Journaling Prompts

Take five minutes (literally!) to jot down your thoughts. Start with prompts like:

- "What's one thing I crushed today?"
- "What makes me proud of myself?"
- "How did I handle something tricky today?"

These are quick and low-pressure but pack a big punch for boosting your mood and mindset. Bonus: Looking back at your journal can be a real eye-opener when you need a confidence boost later.

2. Mind Mapping

Grab some paper, write your name in the center, and draw branches for different parts of your life—school, hobbies, friends, whatever. Under each branch, list the things you're good at. For example, under "school," you might write "creative projects" or "great team player." Seeing your strengths laid out visually can make them feel *real*.

3. Strengths Quizzes

Yep, like a Buzzfeed quiz but actually helpful. Tons of free tools online can help you pinpoint your strengths based on simple questions about your preferences and skills. The results? A personalized list of what makes you amazing, served up on a digital silver platter.

4. Quiet Reflection Time

Find a chill spot, ditch distractions (yes, even TikTok), and just *think*. Ask yourself questions like:

- "What makes me unique?"
- "How did I push through a tough moment this week?"
- "What's one small win I'm proud of?"

This isn't about perfection; it's about getting real with yourself.

Why It's Worth It

When you make self-reflection a habit, you'll notice something magical: your self-talk gets *way* more positive. You'll spot your strengths faster and feel more confident handling challenges. It's like upgrading your inner cheerleader.

Pro Tips to Keep It Up:

- **Set a Reminder:** Add "reflect" to your daily routine, whether it's before bed or during a study break.

- **Make It Fun:** Use colorful pens, doodle in your journal, or turn it into a voice memo if writing isn't your thing.

- **Celebrate Progress:** Reflect on the fact that even taking the time to reflect is a win. High-five yourself (seriously).

Final Thought

Self-reflection is not about being perfect or fixing yourself—it's about recognizing and *celebrating* who you are. ADHD or not, you've got unique strengths that deserve the spotlight. So grab that journal, draw that mind map, or dive into a quiz. Trust me, you'll be amazed at what you discover about yourself.

6.2 Positive Affirmations: Change Your Inner Dialogue, Change Your Life

Let's get real for a second. You wake up, look in the mirror, and say, "I've got this!" It might feel a bit like you're starring in your own cheesy movie, right? But guess what? Positive affirmations are way more powerful than they sound. Think of them as your personal pep squad—showing up every day to cheer you on. The best part? It's all YOU, giving yourself the love and hype you deserve. Trust me, you deserve it! Repeating positive statements like, "I am capable," helps drown out the negativity and bring in a fresh, empowered perspective. Over time, this mindset shift can turn you into the confident, optimistic powerhouse you're meant to be.

Why Affirmations Work (Even if You've Got ADHD)

Living with ADHD is like riding a rollercoaster. Some days you're on top of the world, and other days, you're holding on for dear life with self-doubt creeping in every corner. Here's where affirmations come to the rescue—like mental armor. They protect your mind from those negative thoughts and remind you of all the awesome things that make you, *well, you.* By repeating a simple phrase like "I am resilient," you can train your brain to focus on your strengths. Over time, you'll start believing it—and that belief can help you tackle challenges head-on, without that nagging fear.

Affirmations are like planting seeds. Each time you say one, you're nurturing a little bit of positivity. Before you know it, those seeds grow into a powerful, unshakable mindset.

Creating Your Own Affirmations: Easy, Fun, and Totally Personal

Making affirmations is a piece of cake, and the best part is, they're totally customizable. Here's how you can create ones that really speak to you:

1. **Keep it Positive & Present**: Avoid "I will" statements like "I will be confident." Instead, say, "I am confident." You want to feel like it's already happening.

2. **Focus on Strengths**: Is there something you're working on? Want to feel more organized? Try "I am organized and on top of my game."

3. **Make It a Habit**: Repetition is key! Make it a daily practice. Say them when you wake up, before bed, or whenever you need a quick boost.

Affirmations You Can Totally Steal (or Customize!)

If you need some inspiration, here are a few to get you started:

- "I am proud of what I've accomplished."
- "I am worthy of love and respect."
- "I am a creative problem-solver."
- "I can work at my own pace and still succeed."

Feel free to swap them out or tweak them until they feel like a perfect fit for your vibe. Trust me, it's all about what *resonates* with you—not some cookie-cutter affirmation that makes you cringe every time you say it. And yes, in the beginning, it'll feel a little weird. But that's okay. It's all part of the process! The more you repeat them, the more you'll start to believe them.

Personalizing Your Affirmations: The Secret Sauce

Creating the perfect affirmation doesn't need to be complicated. Here's a simple formula:

1. **Identify a Need or Goal**: What area in your life could use a little positivity boost? Maybe you're feeling overwhelmed with schoolwork or a project at work.
2. Example: "I want to feel more in control of my schoolwork."
3. **Turn it into a Positive Statement**: Flip your struggles into strengths. Instead of "I suck at staying organized," try something like, "I am organized and calm under pressure."
4. Example: "I can tackle any challenge with focus and confidence."
5. **Make It Yours**: If "organized" doesn't feel like your jam, switch it up! Maybe "calm and focused" feels better for you. Keep tweaking until it clicks.

6. Final affirmation: "I approach my responsibilities with calm and focus."

Don't Force It—Find Your Truth

If an affirmation doesn't feel authentic, that's okay! Tweak it until it feels like your truth. If "I am worthy of love" feels out of reach, start with, "I am learning to see my own worth." It's all about progress, not perfection! And trust me, once you find that right affirmation, it'll feel like you're speaking directly to your best self.

Here's a personal favorite of mine: "I don't need to be perfect, I just need to show up." This one felt totally weird at first, like I was setting myself up for failure. But over time, it's become my mantra, a reminder that effort is what counts, not flawlessness.

How to Make Your Affirmations Stick

Here's the secret to sticking with your affirmations:

- **Write them down**: Stick them on your mirror, your phone, or even in your journal. Visual cues are powerful!

- **Say them out loud**: When you hear your own voice saying, "I am enough," it packs a punch. Even if you don't fully believe it yet, say it with *confidence*—fake it 'til you make it!

- **Visualize success**: Close your eyes and picture yourself succeeding, whether it's acing a presentation or staying calm in a stressful situation. Visualization + affirmation = total powerhouse combo!

Why Affirmations Are Worth the Effort

At the end of the day, affirmations aren't just about feeling good (though that's a bonus). They're about rewiring your brain and changing the conversation you have with yourself. Instead of focusing on your flaws or what's hard, affirmations shift your mindset to what's strong, unique, and amazing about you.

So, what are you waiting for? Start small—pick a couple affirmations that resonate with you, and make them part of your daily routine. It may feel weird at first, but don't give up! Stick with it, and you'll soon see how these little words can make a *big* difference. You've got this. And if you don't believe me yet, just repeat after me: "I've got this." Now go out there and prove it!

6.3 Celebrating Small Wins: Why You Shouldn't Skip the Tiny Victories

Ever feel that little rush of excitement when you cross something off your to-do list? That's the magic of celebrating small wins, my friend. It's not just about checking things off; it's about giving yourself a high-five (even if you're alone in your room, it still counts). Acknowledging even the tiniest accomplishments can give you a major confidence boost and keep you going. It's like saying, "Hey, I'm actually getting things done!" and trust me, that feeling? It's addicting.

When you celebrate the little wins, you're telling your brain, "Look, I can do this!" Whether it's finishing a project or just making your bed (no judgment), these small wins build up and create a sense of progress. It's like collecting trophies, but instead of being for sports, they're for adulting. Each small win adds to the bigger picture and helps you stay motivated to keep moving forward.

Now, if you're rocking ADHD (or even if you're just a little overwhelmed by life), celebrating these wins is even more important. Let's be real, ADHD can sometimes feel like a constant reminder of all the things you didn't do. But by celebrating what you *did* accomplish—even if it's as small as remembering to feed your pet—you shift the focus from "ugh, I suck" to "look at me go!" It helps reduce those feelings of failure and frustration and gives you a little mental pep talk to keep pushing. It's like getting a mini win every time you notice how awesome you are.

So, how do you celebrate these small wins? Here are some fun ideas that'll actually help you stay pumped:

1. **Keep a "Wins" Journal**: It's like a diary, but for victories. Write down at least one thing you've accomplished every day. Finished a homework assignment? Boom. Cleared your desk? Heck yes. These wins don't have to be monumental to matter. The goal is to see all the little things adding up.

2. **Share the Good News**: Tell a friend or family member about your accomplishment. It's like telling them, "Hey, I'm totally winning today!" Their encouragement will make it feel real—and might even get you a well-deserved round of applause.

3. **Reward Yourself**: This doesn't have to be big—treat yourself to a piece of chocolate or a five-minute TikTok scroll. You're basically saying, "I worked hard, now I get to relax for a sec."

4. **Visual Progress Tracker**: Create a simple chart or board where you can track your progress. Stickers, stars, or even little notes work great. The more you see your progress grow, the more satisfying it gets. Plus, who doesn't love a good sticker?

Let's look at some examples of small wins you can celebrate:

- **Finished that math assignment on time?** Celebrate!
- **Got your study space organized?** Reward yourself with a quick break or your favorite snack.
- **Managed to speak up in class?** Give yourself a mental high-five.
- **Stuck to a study session without checking your phone every five minutes?** A huge win, seriously.

The key here is not about perfection. It's about acknowledging that every step you take is progress. These small wins create a cycle of motivation and confidence that'll help you crush bigger goals.

So, start today. Keep a journal, share your wins, treat yourself, and track your progress. These tiny victories will make a big difference in how you see yourself and your ability to tackle challenges ahead. Keep stacking those wins, because every step forward is a win worth

celebrating!

6.4 Peer-Validated Success Stories: Learning from Others

Feeling Alone with ADHD? You're Not Alone—And Here's Why

Ever feel like you're the only one struggling with ADHD while everyone else seems to have it all figured out? It's easy to fall into that trap, but guess what? *You're not alone.* Tons of people are navigating the same challenges, and hearing their stories can be a total game-changer. That's where peer-validated success stories come in. These stories aren't just inspiring—they're proof that success is *completely possible,* even with the ups and downs of ADHD.

Hearing how someone else faced similar hurdles and found a way through gives you hope and practical tips you can use in your own life. It's like borrowing a roadmap from someone who's already walked the path you're on. Plus, it's a powerful reminder that you're part of a bigger community—a group of people who understand your struggles and cheer you on every step of the way.

Why Peer Stories Hit Different

For teens and young adults with ADHD, connecting with others who *get it* can be life-changing. When you hear about someone overcoming the same obstacles you're facing, it doesn't just inspire—it reassures you. It's like seeing a flashlight beam cutting through the darkness, showing you that the end of the tunnel is closer than you think.

These stories:

- Help you feel *seen* and less alone.
- Reduce self-doubt by showing that others have succeeded despite similar challenges.
- Offer practical strategies, tools, and ideas that you can actually try.
- Reinforce that your ADHD is just one part of you, not a roadblock to your goals.

Where to Find These Stories

Finding peer success stories is easier than ever. Here are some places to start:

- **Support Groups:** Whether it's in person or online, ADHD support groups are amazing for sharing and hearing personal experiences. You can swap tips, laugh about shared struggles, and cheer each other on.
- **Social Media and YouTube:** Search hashtags like #ADHDSuccess or check out YouTubers sharing their journeys. Many creators post relatable content, strategies, and uplifting stories.
- **Websites and Articles:** Platforms like *ADDitude Magazine* regularly publish stories from people with ADHD, covering everything from school to work to personal growth.
- **Books and Documentaries:** Check out memoirs or documentaries where people share their ADHD experiences. These can be super empowering and insightful.

I know you know this already - but I need to emphasize: be careful when online - only share stories that are safe - what is on the web stays on the web - for ever - so check very carefully what you want to share and with whom---- just saying, I know you know - but, you know, when you get carried away because it feels so good to be understood - use your pause button and reflect what you are disclosing about yourself.

Examples of Real-Life Wins

Here are some success stories that can inspire and motivate you:

- **Academic Comeback:** A student with ADHD who went from struggling in school to acing their classes by using tools like planners, apps, and the Pomodoro Technique. Over time, their grades improved, and so did their confidence.

- **Career Triumph:** A young adult who used their creativity and hyperfocus to build a thriving career, despite struggling with time management. They leaned into their strengths and found work that lets them shine.

- **Social Success:** Someone who struggled with friendships but learned to interpret social cues and joined groups that matched their interests. Over time, they built meaningful relationships and a strong support network.

- **Organizational Wins:** A student who learned to keep track of deadlines using color-coded planners and visual reminders, turning chaos into calm and finding time to actually relax.

Why Sharing Your Story Matters

Success stories aren't just about *reading* them—they're about *sharing* them too. When you talk about your wins (even the small ones), you inspire others and build a sense of community. Your story might be exactly what someone else needs to hear to keep going.

Feeling weird about sharing? Start small. Maybe post a comment on a forum or talk to a friend who's also dealing with ADHD. You'll be surprised how much encouragement and connection comes back your way.

What's Next?

Success isn't about perfection—it's about progress. Whenever you hear or share a story, you build a foundation of hope, resilience, and connection. ADHD might be a part of your story, but it doesn't define you.

So go ahead—seek out those stories, share your own, and remind yourself: You're part of a strong, supportive community, and you've got what it takes to succeed. And remember - I know you know and ah - just be aware of what you are putting on the web...

6.5 Setting Realistic Goals: Achievable Steps Toward Success

Have you ever set a goal that felt so big it was almost impossible to start? Maybe you wanted to improve your grades, but the idea of turning all your Cs into As seemed overwhelming. Setting realistic goals can change that. Realistic goals provide clear direction and purpose, giving you something specific to aim for. They encourage a sense of accomplishment and progress, which builds your confidence bit by bit. When you achieve a goal, no matter how small, it feels good and motivates you to keep going. This focus and motivation help you stay on track and reduce the risk of feeling overwhelmed or discouraged.

For teens with ADHD, setting realistic goals is especially helpful. ADHD can make it hard to break down large tasks into manageable steps. Big, vague goals like "do better in school" can feel like climbing a mountain with no trail to follow. But when you set specific, achievable goals, you create a structured approach to success. This structure encourages consistency and perseverance. Instead of feeling lost, you have a clear plan to follow. Each small step you take builds momentum, making the bigger goal seem more attainable.

Creating realistic goals starts with using the SMART criteria. SMART stands for Specific, Measurable, Achievable, Relevant, and Time-bound. Specific means your goal is clear and detailed. Instead of saying, "I want better grades," say, "I want to improve my math grade to a B." Measurable means you can track your progress. For instance, you could measure your goal by the number of math problems you practice each week. Achievable means your goal is realistic. If you're currently getting a D in math, aiming for an A might be too big a leap; a B is more attainable. Relevant means the goal matters to you. If improving your math grade will help you get into your desired college, it's relevant. Time-bound means you set a deadline. Instead of "someday," you say, "by the end of the semester."

Once you've set a SMART goal, break it down into smaller, actionable steps. For example, if your goal is to improve your math grade, your steps might include: attending extra help sessions, completing all homework assignments, and practicing additional problems for 30 minutes each evening. Regularly review and adjust your goals as needed. Life happens, and sometimes you need to tweak your plan. That's okay. The key is to stay flexible and keep moving forward.

Let's look at some specific examples of realistic goals. Suppose your academic goal is to improve a grade in a specific subject. You might dedicate extra study time each week, like an additional hour for math on Tuesdays and Thursdays. A personal goal could be developing a new hobby or skill. Maybe you want to learn to play the guitar. You could set aside 20 minutes each day to practice. For a social goal, you might aim to make new friends by participating in extracurricular activities. Join a club that interests you and make an effort to attend meetings regularly. An organizational goal could be keeping your study space tidy by decluttering weekly. Spend 15 minutes every Sunday organizing your desk and putting away any stray papers or supplies.

These goals are realistic because they are specific, measurable, achievable, relevant, and time-bound. They break down larger ambitions into smaller, manageable steps, making it easier to stay focused and motivated. By setting and achieving realistic goals, you build confidence and self-esteem. Each small victory reinforces your belief in your ability to succeed, making it easier to tackle the next challenge.

Setting realistic goals helps you take control of your progress and build a sense of accomplishment. By breaking down large tasks into manageable steps, you create a structured path to success. This approach promotes focus, motivation, and consistency, reducing the risk of feeling overwhelmed or discouraged. Start setting your own realistic goals and watch how each small step leads to bigger achievements.

OK, that was a bit long winded; again, short and snappy:

Feeling Overwhelmed? Here's How Realistic Goals Can Help You Crush It

Ever set a goal so huge it felt impossible to even start? Like wanting to turn all your Cs into As, but you didn't know where to begin? That's where *realistic goals* come in. They're like a GPS for your dreams—giving you direction, focus, and purpose. Plus, every time you hit a milestone (big or small), you feel *amazing* and ready to keep going.

For teens with ADHD, realistic goals are game-changers. Big, vague goals like "do better in school" can feel like climbing Mount Everest without a map. Breaking goals into smaller, manageable steps makes them feel doable. Instead of chaos, you've got structure—and with structure comes consistency.

How to Set Goals That Actually Work

The secret sauce? SMART goals. SMART stands for:

- **Specific:** Be clear. Swap "I want better grades" for "I want a B in math."
- **Measurable:** Track your progress. Practice 10 math problems daily, for example.
- **Achievable:** Aim for something realistic. If you're at a D, aim for a C first, not an A.
- **Relevant:** Choose something that matters to *you*, like a better grade for college apps.
- **Time-bound:** Set a deadline, like "by the end of the semester."

Step It Up: Break It Down

Big goals are easier to tackle when broken into bite-sized tasks. If your goal is to improve in math, you could:

- Attend extra help sessions weekly.
- Spend 30 minutes on practice problems each evening.
- Complete homework on time, every time.

Adjust your plan if needed—it's okay to tweak as you go!

Examples to Get You Started

- **Academic Goal:** Boost your math grade by studying 3 extra hours a week and reviewing tests with your teacher.
- **Personal Goal:** Learn guitar by practicing 15 minutes daily.
- **Social Goal:** Join a club and make an effort to chat with one new person per meeting.
- **Organizational Goal:** Keep your desk clean by spending 10 minutes every Sunday decluttering.

Why It Works

Small wins build big confidence. Each tiny step forward proves you *can* do it, and that momentum makes even the scariest goals feel achievable.

So, start now! Set a realistic goal, break it down, and watch those small wins add up to something amazing. You've got this!

Chapter 7

Social Skills and Building Relationships

Imagine you're at a party, and you see a group of friends laughing and chatting effortlessly. You want to join in, but you hesitate because you're not sure how to read the room. Social interactions can be challenging, especially when you have ADHD. It's like trying to navigate a maze where the rules keep changing. But here's the good news: understanding social cues can make a world of difference. Social cues are the unspoken signals people give through their body language, facial expressions, and tone of voice. They help us understand what others are feeling and thinking, even without words. Let's explore how you can get better at reading these cues and improve your social interactions.

7.1 Reading Social Cues: Tips for Better Understanding Others

Understanding social cues is crucial for building and maintaining relationships. These cues include body language, facial expressions, and tone of voice, all of which provide valuable information about others' feelings and intentions. When you can interpret these cues, you can respond appropriately, making your interactions smoother and more meaningful. For instance, if a friend looks away and crosses their arms while you're talking, they might be uncomfortable or disinterested. Recognizing this allows you to adjust your approach, perhaps by changing the topic or asking if something is bothering them. On the other hand, if someone maintains eye contact and leans in while you're speaking, they're likely engaged and interested in what you have to say.

Common social cues and their meanings can sometimes feel like a secret language, but once you learn them, they become easier to recognize. Eye contact, for example, is a powerful indicator of interest and engagement. When someone looks you in the eye, it shows they are paying attention and are genuinely interested in the conversation. Conversely, avoiding eye contact might suggest shyness, discomfort, or disinterest. Facial expressions are another key component. A smile typically indicates happiness or friendliness, while a frown or furrowed brows might signal confusion or displeasure. Pay attention to body language as well. Open postures, such as uncrossed arms and leaning forward, indicate openness and receptiveness, while closed postures, like crossed arms and legs, can suggest defensiveness or discomfort. Lastly, tone of voice adds another layer of meaning. A warm, upbeat tone usually conveys positivity and friendliness, whereas a flat or harsh tone might indicate irritation or boredom.

Improving your ability to read social cues takes practice, but there are some effective strategies to help you get there. One of the best ways is to observe and mimic others. Watch how people interact in different settings, like at school, in movies, or on TV shows. Pay attention to their body language, facial expressions, and tone of voice, and try to mimic these cues in your own interactions. This helps you become more aware of these signals and how they influence communication. Another helpful strategy is to ask for feedback from trusted friends or family. They can provide insights into how you come across and offer suggestions for improvement. Role-playing is also a valuable tool. Engage in role-play scenarios with a friend or family member to practice recognizing and responding to social cues. This can be both fun and educational, giving you a safe space to learn and grow.

Let's look at some specific scenarios to illustrate the importance of social cues. Imagine you're talking to a friend who suddenly becomes quiet and avoids eye contact. Their body language is tense, and they're not contributing much to the conversation. These cues suggest that something might be bothering them. You could acknowledge this by saying, "You seem a bit off today. Is everything okay?" This shows that you're attentive to their feelings and willing to offer support. In another scenario, you're in a group discussion, and you notice someone nodding and maintaining eye contact with you. These signals indicate that they're interested in what you're saying. You can keep the conversation engaging by asking for their opinion or elaborating on the topic. On the flip side, if you notice someone crossing their arms and looking away, it might be a sign of disinterest or discomfort. You could try changing the subject or asking them a question to bring them back into the conversation.

Reading social cues isn't about being perfect; it's about being attentive and responsive. By learning to interpret these signals, you can improve your social interactions and build stronger relationships. It takes practice, but with time, you'll become more adept at understanding and responding to the unspoken language of social cues. So next time you're at a party or in a conversation, pay attention to these cues, and see how they can transform your interactions.

So, in short:

Decode the Secret Language of Social Cues

Ever feel like you're missing something in a conversation? That "something" might be social cues—like body language, facial expressions, and tone of voice. These little signals reveal how someone's feeling and help you respond in the right way.

For example, if your friend crosses their arms and avoids eye contact, they might feel uncomfortable or upset. You can ask, "Is everything okay?" to show you care. But if they're making eye contact and nodding, they're probably super into what you're saying—so keep going!

What to Watch For

- **Eye Contact:** Looking at you = engaged. Avoiding eye contact = shy, distracted, or uncomfortable.
- **Facial Expressions:** A smile = happy or friendly. A frown = confused or upset.
- **Body Language:** Open arms = relaxed and open. Crossed arms = defensive or closed off.
- **Tone of Voice:** Warm and upbeat = friendly. Flat or sharp = annoyed or bored.

How to Get Better at Reading Cues

- **Watch and Learn:** Observe people in real life, TV shows, or movies. Please pay attention to their body language and tone.
- **Practice:** Role-play scenarios with friends or family to test your skills.

- **Ask for Feedback:** Trusted friends can give you tips on how you're doing.

Real-Life Examples

1. **Your Friend Seems Off:** They're quiet, tense, and avoiding eye contact. Say, "Hey, you seem a bit down. Wanna talk?"
2. **Someone's Interested:** They're nodding, leaning in, and holding eye contact. Keep the vibe going by asking their thoughts!
3. **Someone Looks Bored:** They're crossing their arms and glancing away. Switch up the topic or ask them a direct question to re-engage.

> *Pro Tip:* You don't need to be perfect. Just pay attention and adjust. With a little practice, you'll master the unspoken language of social cues—and your connections will get way stronger. Try it out!

7.2 Conversation Starters: How to Break the Ice

Starting a conversation can sometimes feel like standing at the edge of a cold pool, hesitant to jump in. But effective conversation starters can help you break that initial awkwardness, making interactions feel more natural and enjoyable. They act as a bridge, connecting you to the other person and setting the stage for meaningful conversations. Whether you're meeting someone new or catching up with an old friend, good conversation starters can ease the tension and make everyone feel more comfortable.

One of the simplest ways to start a conversation is by offering a genuine compliment. Compliments can instantly put the other person at ease and open up the dialogue. For example, saying, "I really like your backpack! Where did you get it?" not only shows you've noticed something about them but also invites them to share more. Another effective approach is to ask about shared interests. You might say, "What kind of music do you listen to? I'm always looking for new songs." This not only breaks the ice but also helps you find common ground, making the conversation flow more naturally.

Discussing current events or popular topics is another great way to initiate a conversation. You could say, "Did you see the latest episode of that show everyone is talking about?" This not only shows you're up-to-date but also gives the other person an easy topic to jump into. If you're in a school setting, asking questions about classes or projects can be very effective. For instance, "How is your science project going? I'm working on mine too," shows that you're interested in their academic life and can lead to a deeper discussion about shared experiences.

Keeping the conversation going requires a bit of finesse. Active listening is key. Show that you're genuinely interested in what the other person is saying by nodding, maintaining eye contact, and responding thoughtfully. Asking open-ended questions can also encourage more detailed responses. Instead of asking yes-or-no questions, try something like, "What do you like most about your favorite hobby?" This invites the other person to share more about themselves, making the conversation more engaging and meaningful.

Another strategy is to share personal experiences related to the topic at hand. If the other person mentions they enjoy hiking, you might say, "I went hiking last weekend and found this amazing trail. Have you been there?" This not only keeps the conversation going but also makes it more relatable and personal. Balancing the conversation with a mix of questions and shared experiences helps create a two-way dialogue, making the interaction feel more natural and less like an interview.

Let's look at some specific examples of conversation starters and follow-ups.

Imagine you're at a school event and you notice someone with a unique accessory. You could start with, "I really like your necklace! Is there a story behind it?" This not only compliments them but also opens up the conversation. If you're in a group setting and someone mentions a movie, you might say, "What did you think of the movie? I haven't seen it yet, but I'm curious." This shows you're interested in their opinion and encourages them to share more.

In a casual setting, discussing hobbies is always a safe bet. You could ask, "What kind of hobbies do you enjoy? I'm into painting; it's really relaxing." This not only opens up the conversation but also gives them a chance to share their interests, making the interaction more dynamic. Asking about their day is another simple yet effective starter. "How was your day? Did anything exciting happen?" This shows you care about their well-being and can lead to a more in-depth conversation.

Using these techniques makes starting and maintaining conversations a lot easier. The goal is to make the other person feel comfortable and engaged, turning a potentially awkward interaction into a meaningful exchange. So next time you find yourself at the edge of that cold pool, remember these tips and take the plunge. The water's fine.

So, in short to get you started straight away:

How to Dive Into Great Conversations

Starting a conversation can feel awkward, but the right opener makes all the difference. Think of conversation starters as your secret weapon to break the ice and make things flow naturally. Whether meeting someone new or reconnecting, these tips will help you get the convo rolling.

Easy Icebreakers

- **Compliments:** "I love your backpack! Where'd you get it?" Compliments are a great way to show you're paying attention and invite a response.

- **Shared Interests:** "What kind of music are you into? I'm looking for new recs!" Finding common ground makes talking so much easier.

- **Current Topics:** "Did you catch the latest episode of [insert popular show]?" Talking about trends keeps things fun and relatable.

- **School or Work:** "How's your science project going? Mine's a work in progress!" Shared experiences make for natural conversations.

Keep It Going

1. **Listen Actively:** Nod, make eye contact, and show genuine interest.

2. **Ask Open-Ended Questions:** Instead of "Do you like hiking?" try "What's your favorite hiking spot?" You want a question that they can't answer with a yes or no - that could shut down the conversation straight away - especially when you are dealing with another ADHD brain :)

3. **Share Your Stories:** If they mention something like hiking, jump in with, "I found a cool trail last weekend—ever been there?"

Quick Starters

- Compliment their style: "That necklace is awesome! Is there a story behind it?"
- Ask about hobbies: "What do you do for fun? I've been getting into painting—it's so chill."
- Check in on their day: "How's your day going? Anything fun happen?"

With these tips, even the most awkward starts can turn into meaningful exchanges. Don't overthink it—just take the plunge and see where the conversation takes you. You got this!

7.3 Maintaining Friendships: The Art of Keeping in Touch

Friendships are like plants; they need regular care and attention to thrive. When you consistently stay in touch with your friends, you build trust and closeness, making your relationships stronger. This consistent communication fosters a sense of connection and belonging, which is crucial for everyone, especially when you have ADHD. It gives you a support system where you can share your highs and lows, knowing that someone is there to listen and understand. Keeping in touch doesn't have to be complicated or time-consuming. Small, consistent efforts can make a big difference.

One practical way to maintain friendships is by scheduling regular meet-ups or hangouts. Whether it's a weekly movie night, a monthly game session, or just grabbing coffee, having these plans in place shows that you value the relationship. It gives both of you something to look forward to and ensures that you're making time for each other despite busy schedules. Another great way to stay connected is by using social media and messaging apps. These platforms make it easy to send a quick message, share a funny meme, or update each other on your lives. A simple "How's your day going?" or "Check out this article, it reminded me of you!" can go a long way in maintaining the bond.

Sending thoughtful messages or small gifts on special occasions is another effective strategy. Birthdays, anniversaries, or even random days can be great opportunities to show your friends that you care. A heartfelt message or a small gift doesn't have to be extravagant; it's the thought that counts. For instance, if you know your friend loves a particular band, sending them a link to a new song or a concert announcement can make their day. These small gestures show that you're thinking of them and appreciate their presence in your life.

Balancing effort in friendships is crucial. It's important to ensure that both parties contribute to the relationship. Friendships should be a two-way street, where both of you make an effort to stay connected and support each other. Be considerate of each other's schedules and commitments. If your friend is swamped with exams or work, give them some space but also let them know you're there when they need a break. Being understanding and flexible helps in maintaining a healthy balance, ensuring that the friendship doesn't feel like a burden to either of you.

Planning a weekly movie night or game session is a fun and effective way to keep in touch. It gives you a regular activity to look forward to and strengthens your bond through shared experiences. You could take turns choosing the movie or game, adding an element of surprise and excitement. Sending a quick text to check in and ask how their day was can also make a big difference. It shows that you care about their well-being and are interested in their daily life. Remembering and celebrating birthdays and other milestones is another great way to show you care. A simple "Happy Birthday!" message or a small gift can make your friend feel special and appreciated.

Sharing interesting articles or memes that remind you of your friend is another easy way to maintain the connection. If you come across something that you think they'll enjoy or find funny, send it to them with a quick note. It shows that you're thinking of them and value their sense of humor or interests. These small acts of thoughtfulness can brighten their day and keep the friendship alive and well.

Maintaining friendships takes effort, but it's worth it. You can strengthen your relationships and build a supportive network by staying in touch, planning regular meet-ups, and being thoughtful. Friendships provide a sense of belonging and support, making life's challenges a bit easier to handle. So, take a moment to reach out to your friends, plan that hangout, and send that thoughtful message. Your friendships will thank you for it.

In summary: How to Keep Friendships Alive

Friendships are like plants—they need regular care to grow. Staying in touch strengthens your bond, builds trust, and creates a support system where you can share the highs and lows of life, especially if you have ADHD. And guess what? It doesn't have to be complicated!

Simple Ways to Stay Connected

- **Plan Hangouts:** Weekly movie nights, monthly game sessions, or quick coffee meetups give you both something fun to look forward to.

- **Use Social Media & Texts:** A quick "How's your day?" or sharing a meme that made you laugh can keep the connection strong.

- **Celebrate Special Moments:** Remember birthdays or milestones with a thoughtful message or small gift—it's the thought that counts!

Keep the Balance

Friendship is a two-way street. Both of you should pitch in to stay connected. Be understanding if your friends are busy, but let them know you're there when they're ready to catch up.

Little Things, Big Impact

- Share articles or memes that remind you of them.
- Be there with encouragement or a listening ear.
- Make consistent, small efforts to show you care.

Friendships don't thrive by accident—they grow with effort, thoughtfulness, and shared moments. So send that text, plan that hangout, and keep watering those friendship plants—you'll be glad you did! 🌱 ✨

7.4 Navigating Social Media: Using Platforms Wisely

Imagine scrolling through your social media feed and seeing posts from friends, family, and influencers. It's a mixed bag of funny memes, vacation photos, and the latest trends. Social media is a powerful tool that helps you stay connected with friends and family, even when you're miles apart. It provides a platform for self-expression, allowing you to share your thoughts, creativity, and experiences with the world. But while social media has its perks, it also comes with pitfalls that you must navigate carefully.

Using social media wisely can enhance social interactions without negative consequences. It's all about balance. On the positive side, social media allows you to connect with like-minded individuals and share your experiences. You can join groups or follow hashtags related to your interests, finding communities that resonate with you. This can be incredibly validating, especially if you feel like you don't fit in at school or in your local community. Sharing your thoughts, art, or achievements can also boost your confidence and give you a sense of belonging.

However, social media isn't all sunshine and rainbows. One of the biggest risks is cyberbullying. Negative comments and online harassment can have a significant impact on your mental health. It's essential to be aware of this and know how to handle it if it occurs. Another downside is the constant comparison. Seeing others' highlight reels can make you feel inadequate or like you're missing out. This social comparison can lead to feelings of jealousy, low self-esteem, and even depression. Additionally, social media can be a major distraction, pulling you away from your responsibilities and affecting your productivity.

Setting time limits is important to using social media responsibly. It's easy to lose track of time when scrolling through endless posts. Try setting a timer for 30 minutes a day to limit your screen time. This helps you stay connected without letting social media take over your life. Another strategy is to curate a positive and supportive online environment. Follow accounts that promote positivity and inspiration. If you come across individuals who engage in negative behavior or spread toxicity, don't hesitate to unfollow or block them. Your mental well-being is more important than the number of followers you have.

Being mindful of privacy settings and shared content is also essential. Regularly review and adjust your privacy settings to ensure that only people you trust can see your posts. Be cautious about sharing personal information, such as your location, phone number, or other sensitive details. Think twice before posting anything that could be misinterpreted or used against you. Remember, once something is online, it's challenging to take it back.

Let's look at some specific examples of responsible social media practices. Limiting screen time to 30 minutes per day can help you stay focused on your tasks and reduce the time spent comparing yourself to others. Following accounts that promote positivity and inspiration can uplift your mood and provide a sense of community. For instance, follow pages that share motivational quotes, mental health tips, or creative content. If you encounter negativity, don't hesitate to unfollow or block individuals who engage in harmful behavior. This creates a safer and more positive online environment for you.

Reviewing and adjusting your privacy settings regularly is another crucial practice. Make it a habit to check your privacy settings once a month to ensure that your information is secure. Be mindful of the content you share, and avoid posting anything that could compromise your safety or privacy. If you're unsure about a post, ask yourself if you'd be comfortable with your family, teachers, or future employers seeing it. If the answer is no, it's best to keep it private.

Navigating social media wisely requires a balance of staying connected and protecting your mental well-being. By setting time limits, curating a positive environment, and being mindful of privacy, you can enjoy the benefits of social media without falling into its traps.

So, in short:

Social media is a great way to stay connected with friends and family, share your creativity, and discover new trends. But it's important to use it wisely! There's a balance to strike between staying social and protecting your mental well-being.

On the plus side, social media helps you find communities that share your interests and boosts your confidence when you post about your passions. But it can also be a source of stress. Cyberbullying, comparison, and distractions are real risks, so it's important to set limits. Try limiting screen time to 30 minutes a day, follow accounts that inspire you, and unfollow anything or anyone spreading negativity.

Privacy matters too! Keep your settings updated, and think carefully before posting anything personal or controversial. With a little mindfulness, you can enjoy the fun parts of social media while avoiding the downsides. Stay connected, stay positive, and stay safe online!

7.4 Building Your Support Squad: Finding Friends Who Get You

Your Ultimate Guide to Building an Awesome Support Squad

Having a solid crew of friends is like having your own personal cheerleading team—they're there to catch you when you stumble and hype you up when you crush it. When your friends truly get you, it's like having a safety net for life's ups and downs, especially if you're navigating ADHD. A supportive circle can boost your confidence, help you grow, and turn even the roughest days into something brighter.

Finding Your People

Sure, making new friends can feel intimidating, but guess what? It's totally doable! Start by joining clubs, teams, or groups that match your interests. Whether you're into soccer, drama, anime, or book clubs, these are perfect places to meet people who vibe with your passions.

Want to expand your circle even more? Hit up school events, community meetups, or volunteer gigs. These spots are great for connecting with kind, empathetic people who might just become lifelong friends.

Building Strong Friendships

Great friendships don't just happen—they're built on trust and mutual support. Be someone your friends can count on by following through on promises and showing up when they need you. Celebrate their wins, support them during tough times, and don't be afraid to lean on them when you're struggling too.

Pro tip: honesty goes a long way. Let your friends know if ADHD is making life tricky. Most of the time, they'll appreciate your openness and may even have advice to share.

Real-Life Ways to Grow Your Squad

- **Join clubs or sports teams**: Regular meetups and practices mean you'll naturally spend time bonding with teammates.
- **Get involved in your community**: Volunteer or attend local events to meet people with similar values and interests.
- **Find peers who relate**: Support groups or online communities can connect you with others who really understand what you're going through.

The Power of Being Real

Friendships thrive when you're willing to be vulnerable and open. Sharing your struggles—and being there when your friends share theirs—creates deep, meaningful connections. Show them you're invested in the relationship, and they'll do the same for you.

Why It's Totally Worth It

Building your crew takes time, but trust me—it's 100% worth the grind. When you've got friends who really *get* you, handling ADHD (and life!) feels way less overwhelming. They'll lift you up, cheer you on, and remind you that you're never alone.

So, take the leap! Whether it's joining a club, saying "yes" to that invite, or sliding into a new group chat, your dream squad is out there, ready to make your world brighter.

Now that you're on your way to mastering friendships, let's keep the glow-up going! Next up: learning how to crush decision-making and prioritization like a pro. Let's do this! 🌱 ✨

Chapter 8

Decision-Making and Prioritization Skills

8.1 Decision Fatigue

Feeling Decision Overload? Here's How to Beat It

Ever stared at a menu and felt like picking between a cheeseburger and a salad was *the* hardest decision of your life? Yep, that's **decision fatigue**—and it's totally real, especially if you've got ADHD. Think of your brain like a phone battery: every decision you make drains a little power. By the end of the day, even tiny choices can feel impossible. Let's break it down and learn how to handle it like a pro.

What's Decision Fatigue?

It's what happens when your brain gets overworked from too many decisions, kind of like your muscles after a tough workout. The more choices you make, the harder it gets to keep going. Suddenly, small things like picking an outfit or deciding what to eat feel *huge*.

Here's the deal:

- **You get impulsive**: Grabbing the first thing you see or saying "yes" without thinking.
- **You avoid choices**: Just skipping decisions altogether because it's too much.
- **You feel wiped out**: Mental exhaustion kicks in, making everything feel frustrating or overwhelming.

How to Outsmart Decision Fatigue

Good news: you can totally take control with a few simple hacks!

1. **Simplify Your Options**
   - **Capsule wardrobe**: Pick a few versatile clothing pieces that mix and match. Now, you've got easy outfits on repeat—no stress, no overthinking.
   - **Meal prep**: Spend a couple of hours over the weekend planning and prepping your meals. Boom—no more daily "What's for dinner?" panic.

2. **Build Routines**
   - Turn the repetitive stuff into autopilot mode.
   - Create a **morning routine**: Wake up, brush your teeth, grab breakfast, and glance at your schedule—all without needing to decide what's next.
   - Stick to habits: Once something's a habit, it's one less thing to think about!

3. **Tackle Big Decisions Early**
   - Your brain's sharpest in the morning, so handle important stuff first. Whether it's planning a

project or deciding which assignment to start, morning-you makes better choices than end-of-the-day-you.

Real-Life Hacks to Save Brain Power

- **Plan ahead**: Decide tonight what you'll wear and eat tomorrow. Morning-you will thank you.

- **Batch decisions**: Group similar choices together. For example, plan your outfits or meals for the whole week in one go.

- **Automate where you can**: Use tools like calendar reminders or apps to reduce decision-making on the fly.

By keeping things simple, building routines, and prioritizing decisions when your brain's fresh, you'll dodge that decision fatigue and feel way more in control. Save your energy for what really matters—and enjoy the extra brainpower!

8.2 The Eisenhower Matrix: Prioritizing Tasks Effectively

I can not stress enough just how much this relatively simple technique changed my life!

Imagine sitting down to tackle your to-do list and feeling overwhelmed by the sheer number of tasks staring back at you. You're not sure where to start, so you end up doing the easiest things first or, worse, nothing at all. This is where the Eisenhower Matrix can be the next level saver. Named after Dwight D. Eisenhower, the 34th President of the United States, this matrix helps you sort tasks based on their urgency and importance. It divides tasks into four categories: Urgent & Important, Not

Urgent & Important, Urgent & Not Important, and Not Urgent & Not Important. By categorizing tasks, you can see at a glance what needs your immediate attention and what can wait, making it easier to focus on what truly matters.

For people with ADHD, the Eisenhower Matrix is particularly useful because it provides a clear visual representation of what's important and what's not. Go ahead - search images of the Eisenhower matrix on line and use the one that most appeals to you visually. It helps break down overwhelming tasks into manageable categories, reducing the stress of trying to do everything at once. When you can see your tasks laid out in front of you, it's easier to prioritize and focus on the most critical ones. This structured approach can make a world of difference in managing your time and staying on top of your responsibilities.

So, how do you use the Eisenhower Matrix? Start by listing all your tasks. Don't worry about categorizing them yet; just get everything down on paper. Once you have your list, divide it into four quadrants: Urgent & Important, Not Urgent & Important, Urgent & Not Important, and Not Urgent & Not Important. Tasks in the Urgent & Important quadrant are your top priority. These are things that need to be done immediately and have significant consequences if not completed. Focus on these tasks first. Next, look at the Not Urgent & Important quadrant. These tasks are crucial but don't have immediate deadlines. Schedule time to work on these tasks regularly to ensure they don't become urgent. Tasks in the Urgent & Not Important quadrant are often distractions that seem urgent but aren't critical. Delegate these tasks if possible or set aside specific times to deal with them. Finally, tasks in the Not Urgent & Not Important quadrant are your lowest priority. These are often time-wasters that can be eliminated or done during downtime.

Let's see how this works with real-life examples. Say you have school assignments, extracurricular activities, and daily chores. Start by listing everything you need to do. For school assignments, categorize them based on due dates and importance. A math assignment due tomorrow would go in the Urgent & Important quadrant. A long-term project due next month would go in Not Urgent & Important. For extracurricular activities, practices and events with fixed dates might be Urgent & Important. Planning for an upcoming club meeting might be Not Urgent & Important. Daily chores like taking out the trash could be Urgent & Not Important, while organizing your bookshelf might fall into Not Urgent & Not Important.

Now, prioritize your daily chores and responsibilities. Taking out the trash could be Urgent & Not Important—it needs to be done but isn't critical. Cleaning your room might be Not Urgent & Important, something to schedule regularly. Tasks like scrolling through social media or playing video games might fall into the Not Urgent & Not Important category. These activities can be done during downtime or as a reward after completing more critical tasks.

Managing long-term projects and deadlines becomes more manageable with the Eisenhower Matrix. Break down a large project into smaller tasks and categorize them. Researching for a paper might be Urgent & Important as the deadline approaches, while gathering materials could be Not Urgent & Important. Schedule regular check-ins to ensure you're making progress and adjust your priorities as needed.

The Eisenhower Matrix simplifies decision-making and task management by providing a clear visual layout of what's important and urgent. This structure helps you focus on what truly matters and reduces the overwhelm that comes from trying to juggle multiple tasks. Whether it's school assignments, extracurriculars, or daily chores, the Eisenhower Matrix can help you stay organized and on top of your responsibilities.

So once again to make it stick:

Let's say you've got a bunch of stuff to do: homework, chores, and scrolling through TikTok. Here's how you'd use the Eisenhower Matrix to make sense of it:

1. **Urgent & Important**: Homework that's due tomorrow (like a math assignment) – this needs to get done ASAP!

2. **Not Urgent & Important**: A project that's due in two weeks – still important, but not urgent. Plan a little bit each day.

3. **Urgent & Not Important**: Taking out the trash – it needs to be done, but it's not a big deal if it's delayed a bit. Maybe delegate it or set a time to do it later.

4. **Not Urgent & Not Important**: Scrolling on social media – fun, but not a priority right now. Do it after you've finished everything else!

Now, you've got a clear roadmap: Focus on homework, work on your project over time, handle your chores, and leave social media for when you've earned it!

8.3 Making Quick Decisions: Trusting Your Gut

Master the Art of Quick Decisions and Trusting Your Gut

Ever spent *way* too long picking what to eat, only to end up stressed out instead of satisfied? Quick decision-making can be a total game-changer, especially when your schedule's packed. When you decide fast, you dodge overthinking, avoid procrastination, and feel way more in control. Plus, every swift choice builds confidence and clears your mind for the big stuff.

What's the Deal with Gut Feelings?

Your "gut feeling" is like your brain's superpower—it's an instant reaction based on past experiences and subconscious knowledge. It's not magic; it's your intuition, and it's surprisingly accurate for small, everyday choices. While some situations need careful thought, trusting your gut is a lifesaver when time is tight.

Think of it this way: overanalyzing what to eat or wear isn't worth the brainpower. Rely on your gut for quick, low-stakes decisions, and save the deep thinking for stuff that *really* matters.

How to Decide Fast and Stress-Free

1. **Set Time Limits**

    Give yourself a timer—five minutes to pick an outfit, two minutes to choose what to eat. When the timer's up, make the call and move on. Boom, decision made.

2. **Use the Two-Minute Rule**

    If a decision takes less than two minutes, just do it. No debate, no delay. This trick stops small choices from piling up and overwhelming you.

3. **Start Small**

    Practice with no-pressure decisions, like choosing a snack or what to watch. The more you flex your decision-making muscle, the stronger it gets.

Quick Decisions in Action

- **School Projects**: Stuck picking a topic? Set a 10-minute timer, list a few ideas, and choose the one that pops out. Trust your first instinct—it's usually spot on.

- **What to Wear**: Don't let your closet turn into a battlefield. Set a timer, grab what feels right, and own it. No second-guessing required.

- **Ordering Food**: Menus are overwhelming? Give yourself two minutes to scan, pick what looks good, and roll with it. Your first choice is probably the one you'll enjoy most anyway.

By practicing these strategies, quick decision-making will start to feel like second nature. Trust your gut, set limits, and don't sweat the small stuff. You'll feel less stressed, make choices faster, and have more energy for the things that *really* matter. Whether it's picking a meal, an outfit, or a project, you've got this!

The short version to make it stick:

A "gut feeling" is that instinctive hunch or vibe you get about something—it's like your body's built-in compass. You can't always explain it, but you *just* know something feels right (or wrong). It's your brain picking up on clues you might not even be aware of.

How to use it? Trust it! If something feels off, pay attention and take a step back. If you feel excited and confident about a decision, go for it. Just remember: while gut feelings are helpful, don't ignore logic and facts—use both to make the best call!

8.4 How to Balance School and Social Life Without Losing Your Mind

Balancing school and a social life can feel like a circus act. On one side, there's homework, exams, and projects. On the other, there's friends, hobbies, and all the fun stuff you don't want to miss. Striking the right balance is key—it keeps you happy, avoids burnout, and makes life way less stressful.

Time Blocking: Your Secret Weapon

Time blocking is a lifesaver for managing both school and social plans. Here's how to nail it:

1. **Map Your Priorities:** List your must-dos, like classes, study time, and sports.

2. **Block Your Time:** Divide your day into chunks. Example: 8 AM–3 PM for school, 3 PM–5 PM for homework, 5 PM–7 PM for friends.

3. **Stick to It:** Make time for work *and* play. Your schedule is your game plan!

Set Boundaries Like a Boss

Don't let one side take over—set clear boundaries.

- **For School:** Let friends know when you're in study mode and can't hang out.

- **For Fun:** Schedule breaks so you don't drown in assignments. Work hard, play hard, and protect both sides of your life.

Prioritize What Matters Most

Not all tasks are created equal.

1. **List It Out:** Write down everything you need to do.
2. **Rank by Importance:** Tackle the big stuff first—like tomorrow's assignment or that huge project.
3. **Work Smart:** Once the heavy lifting is done, move on to smaller tasks.

Build a Balanced Schedule

Keep your week running smoothly:

- **Busy Week?** Plan study sessions and hangouts ahead. Example: Study Monday/Wednesday, chill Tuesday/Thursday.
- **Weekend Balance:** Sports practice Saturday morning, homework in the afternoon, and Sunday for relaxing.

Don't Skip Downtime

You're not a machine—schedule time to recharge.

- Take short breaks during study sessions.
- Do something fun, like listening to music or going for a walk.
- Relaxing helps you stay focused and stress-free.

Balancing school and social life doesn't have to be a struggle. Use time blocking, set boundaries, prioritize like a pro, and make room for rest. You'll stay on top of your game *and* have time for what makes you happy. You've got this!

8.5 Dodging Time Traps: How to Crush Distractions

Let's get real about time traps—the sneaky little thieves that eat your hours and leave you wondering where your day went. You know the drill: you sit down to study, but somehow you're 47 TikToks deep or on a gaming marathon. Social media, endless gaming, and multitasking (but finishing nothing) are classic culprits. They seem harmless at first but quickly turn your productive vibe into chaos. Recognizing these traps is your first step toward kicking them to the curb.

Why Time Traps Hit Hard (Especially with ADHD)

If you've got ADHD, time traps are even trickier. Here's the deal:

- **Social Media Rabbit Holes:** Five minutes of scrolling turns into an hour before you know it.
- **Procrastination Games:** Telling yourself "later" feels good now but brings panic later.
- **Task-Hopping:** Starting homework, switching to texts, and getting nothing done—it's a spiral.

Not only do these traps waste time, but they also crank up your stress when deadlines sneak up.

Take Back Your Time: Spot and Stop Time Traps

1. **Track It:** Write down where your hours go. Seriously, do it for a day—it'll blow your mind.
2. **Set Limits:** Love social media? Cool, but cap it at 15 minutes in the morning and night. Stick to it!

3. **Use Tools:** Apps like RescueTime show exactly how much time you're spending online. Spoiler: it's more than you think.

Build Your Focus Fortress

- **Kill Notifications:** They're tiny monsters that keep pulling you away. Mute 'em.
- **Study Zone Only:** Find a quiet space and keep your phone *out of reach*.
- **Work in Sprints:** Try 30 minutes of focus, then take a 5-minute TikTok break. Reward yourself without derailing your flow.

Real-Life Hacks for Beating Distractions

- **Scenario 1: The History Test Cram**
- Studying but keep reaching for your phone? Use RescueTime to block social apps. Set a 30-minute timer to study, then take 5 to scroll guilt-free. Boom—productivity and fun.
- **Scenario 2: Scrolling Gone Wild**
- Before opening Instagram, set a 15-minute timer. When it buzzes, *stop scrolling*. No exceptions. You'll still catch the memes without losing hours.
- **Scenario 3: Project Mode**
- Find a distraction-free zone, turn off notifications, and only keep what you need nearby. No random tabs, no doom scrolling. Focus, finish, and celebrate after.

Win the Day by Owning Your Time

The key to dodging time traps? Stay aware of how you spend your time and take charge. Track it, set limits, and build systems to help you focus. Whether you're studying, working on a project, or just keeping up with daily tasks, avoiding distractions keeps you in control and stress-free.

You've got the tools—now it's time to crush your goals and make the most of every hour. Let's move on to building solid support systems to help you stay winning!

Chapter 9

Parental and Educator Involvement

Imagine you're trying to explain why you haven't finished your homework. You're frustrated, your parents are frustrated, and it feels like no one is really hearing you. Sound familiar? Effective communication is key to bridging this gap. It's not just about talking; it's about understanding and being understood. When communication is clear and empathetic, it can improve relationships and provide the support you need to thrive with ADHD.

9.1 How to Get Your Parents (or Another Adult) to *Actually* Listen to You

Let's be real: talking to parents or other adults can sometimes feel like trying to explain TikTok trends to someone who still thinks Facebook is cool. But good communication is *key* if you want them to get where you're coming from. Plus, it's not just about dumping your feelings out—it's about building trust and solving problems together. Here's how to make those chats smoother, less awkward, and maybe even...productive.

Step 1: Help Them *Really* Hear You

You know when you're venting about something, and they jump in with advice or, worse, a lecture? Yeah, not helpful. Teach them about *active listening* by showing them what works. Start by saying, "Hey, I just need you to listen for a sec, not solve this." Most adults aren't mind-readers, so setting the vibe helps.

> ***Pro Tip :*** *If they say something like, "So you're stressed about your math project?"—even if it's obvious—don't roll your eyes. That's them trying to understand. Reward them with a simple, "Yeah, exactly!" It'll encourage them to keep listening instead of going into fix-it mode.*

Step 2: Don't Let Them Interrupt Your TED Talk

Ever start explaining something, and they cut you off with, "Well, back in my day..."? Shut it down (nicely). Say, "Can I finish my thought first?" If you keep calm, they're more likely to zip it and let you talk.

And if they're giving off "I'm just nodding to be polite" vibes? Watch their non-verbal cues. Make eye contact (even if it's awkward), and ask, "Does that make sense?" You'll force them to stay in the moment instead of mentally planning their next grocery list.

Step 3: Teach Them the Magic of "I" Statements

Nobody likes feeling blamed, and that includes adults. If they're coming at you with "You never clean your room!" vibes, you're going to tune out. Suggest they use "I" statements instead.

For example, say: "It's easier to talk if you say stuff like, 'I feel stressed when the room's messy,' instead of making it sound like an attack." Not only does this keep the convo chill, but it also makes you look like a mature genius. Bonus points for that.

Step 4: Open-Ended Questions FTW

Closed questions are the conversation killers of the universe. If they're asking, "Did you do your homework?" you're gonna mumble "yes" (or maybe "uhhh...kinda"). But if they ask, "What's stressing you out about homework this week?"—now we're talking.

Next time, steer them towards open-ended questions by saying, "Can you ask me what I think about this instead of just 'yes' or 'no' stuff? It helps me explain better." It's like giving them cheat codes to better convos.

Step 5: Make It a Judgment-Free Zone

No one wants to talk to someone who's gonna freak out the moment you get real. If you're nervous about saying something, start with, "I need to tell you something, but I need you to not freak out, okay?" Setting that boundary up front can make a huge difference.

And if they do go into panic mode? Calmly remind them: "I need you to listen, not react. Let's solve this *together*." Adults love feeling included, so this line is gold.

Step 6: Use Humor to Break the Ice

Conversations can get heavy, so lighten the mood when you can. If they're lecturing you, try saying, "Whoa, am I getting a life lesson right now? Should I take notes?" It might make them laugh—and laughter equals less tension.

Why This All Matters

Getting adults to listen isn't just about getting what you want (though, let's be honest, that's a nice bonus). It's about creating a connection. When you can actually talk things out, it builds trust, making tackling stuff—like ADHD challenges or just life in general—a whole lot easier.

Remember, communication is a two-way street. They're not perfect, and neither are you, but practicing these tips makes things smoother. Plus, once they see how much better things are when they actually listen, they might try harder.

Bottom Line: Treat communication like building a bridge. Start with small steps, keep it sturdy, and before you know it, you've got a solid path to real talk. Boom. You're a pro.

To make communication even more effective, here are a few tips:

Communication Exercise: Reflective Listening Practice

1. **Sit down with a parent or educator**: Choose a quiet time to practice.

2. **Share a concern**: Speak about something that's been on your mind.

3. **Parent/Educator Reflects**: They should paraphrase what you said to show understanding.

4. **Discuss how it felt**: Discuss how the exercise made you feel and what you learned.

This exercise helps both parties practice listening and understanding, which can improve communication over time. By making an effort to communicate effectively, parents and educators can provide the support you need to thrive. Communication isn't just about talking; it's about connecting and understanding each other. With the right tools and techniques, you can build stronger, more supportive relationships.

9.2 Creating a Supportive Environment at Home

Living with ADHD can feel like navigating a maze where the walls keep shifting. Having a supportive home environment can make a world of difference. A nurturing and structured home provides stability and predictability, which are like guardrails that keep you on track. This stability helps you develop positive behaviors and habits, making daily life feel less chaotic. When your surroundings are predictable, it reduces stress and anxiety, allowing you to focus better and feel more at ease.

Establishing routines and structure is one of the most effective ways to create this supportive environment. It might sound boring, but having regular meal and sleep times can work wonders. When you eat and sleep at the same times every day, your body gets into a rhythm, making it easier to concentrate and stay alert. Creating a daily schedule for schoolwork and chores also helps. Knowing what you need to do and when takes the guesswork out of the day, making it easier to stay on top of tasks. Using visual aids like calendars and charts can make this even more effective. Imagine a colorful chart on your wall that shows your daily tasks. It's a constant reminder of what needs to be done, helping you stay organized without feeling overwhelmed.

Setting up a distraction-free study space is another crucial aspect. Choose a quiet and well-lit area where you can focus without interruptions. This might be a corner of your room or a spot in the living room away from the TV. Removing unnecessary distractions is key. Turn off the TV, limit noise, and keep your phone out of reach while you study. Organize your study materials and supplies so everything you need is easily accessible. A clean, organized space helps clear your mind, making it easier to concentrate on your work.

Providing emotional support is equally important. Living with ADHD can be frustrating, and having someone who understands and empathizes with your struggles can make a big difference. Being empathetic and validating your feelings shows that your family gets what you're going through. It's reassuring to know that someone understands your challenges. Encouraging open communication about your struggles and concerns is crucial. You should feel comfortable talking about what's bothering you without fear of judgment. Offering encouragement and reassurance can help boost your confidence. Hearing "You're doing great" or "I'm proud of you" can be incredibly motivating, especially on tough days.

Creating a supportive environment isn't just about physical space; it's about emotional and mental support too. When your home feels like a safe haven where you're understood and supported, it becomes easier to manage the challenges of ADHD. It's like having a solid foundation that keeps you grounded, allowing you to focus on your goals and thrive.

For a more interactive approach, try this:

Home Environment Checklist

1. **Set Regular Times**: Establish consistent meal and sleep times.
2. **Create a Daily Schedule**: Use a planner or a wall chart to list daily tasks.
3. **Choose a Study Area**: Pick a quiet, well-lit spot for studying.

4. **Remove Distractions**: Keep the study area free from noise and unnecessary items.

5. **Organize Supplies**: Ensure all study materials are easily accessible.

6. **Validate Feelings**: Show empathy and understanding towards challenges.

7. **Encourage Openness**: Foster an environment where you can talk freely about your concerns.

8. **Offer Reassurance**: Regularly provide words of encouragement and praise.

By following this checklist, you can create a home environment that supports your needs and helps you navigate the challenges of ADHD with more ease and confidence.

9.3 How to Team Up with Your Teachers and Win at School

Let's be real: sitting in class and zoning out happens to the best of us. But wouldn't it be awesome if your teachers actually understood *you*—like, they know you need more time on a test or that PowerPoint slides make way more sense than listening to a lecture? Building that connection takes teamwork, and you're a big part of that squad. Here's how to get your parents, teachers, and even yourself working together to make school less of a struggle and more of a win.

1. Keep Everyone in the Loop

Think of it like a group chat (minus the memes): your parents and teachers need to stay updated about what's working and what's not. Suggest that they have regular check-ins—kind of like a team meeting for your success.

Your Move:

- Ask for monthly email updates or quick chats with your teacher. A simple, "Hey, how do you think I'm doing?" shows you're interested and keeps the convo going.

- Use a shared notebook, app, or even a Google Doc to track what's working, where you're struggling, and any cool wins (like that time you aced the quiz you thought would crush you).

2. Let Teachers Know How You Learn Best

Here's the deal: teachers don't know what's in your brain unless you tell them. Are you a visual learner? Do written instructions help more than verbal ones? Share that info with them so they can tweak how they teach you.

Pro Tip: If talking to them feels awkward, prep a cheat sheet with your parents. Write down stuff like:

- What helps you focus (like sitting in the front or using noise-canceling headphones).

- What throws you off (looking at you, group work without clear instructions).

Hand it over at the start of the year, or drop them an email with a "Hey, here's some stuff that helps me learn!" They'll appreciate the heads-up, and you'll look super organized.

3. Speak Up for Yourself

Advocating for what you need doesn't have to be scary. If extra test time, breaks during class, or a quieter spot to work would help, ask for it. Teachers usually *want* to help—they just need to know how.

What to Say:

- "I've noticed I focus better when I can take quick breaks. Can we work that into class?"
- "I'm having a hard time keeping up with notes. Could I get a copy of the slides or an outline?"

Practice saying these things at home if it makes you less nervous. You can even team up with your parents to back you up if needed.

4. Get the Inside Scoop on IEPs and 504 Plans

If you've got an IEP or 504 Plan (a customized learning plan), make sure you know what's in it. These plans are there to give you a fair shot at school, like allowing extra time on tests or seating you away from distractions.

How to Crush It:

- Before the meeting, list things that help or challenges you're facing.
- Speak up during the meeting—yes, you! Say, "It helps when…" or "I think I need more support with…"
- Afterward, make sure your teacher is actually following the plan. If not, gently remind them. ("Hey, my IEP says I get extended test time. Can we make sure that happens?")

5. Make Communication Easier for Everyone

Let's face it: parents and teachers sometimes have their own awkwardness when talking to each other. Make it smoother by suggesting a communication log. It's like a shared diary about you (minus the drama).

How to Use It:

- Your parents can write stuff like, "They had a rough week, so they might need extra help."
- Your teacher can jot down wins, like, "Great participation in class today!"
- You can even add your own notes: "Can we try using more videos in class? They help me understand better."

6. Build a Team, Not a Tug-of-War

When parents and teachers are on the same page, it's way less stressful for you. But you can help keep things chill, too. If there's an issue, try saying, "Can we all work together to figure this out?" Boom. Instant mediator.

And for those of you who are already in the workplace:

9.4 Teaming Up with Your Boss: How to Succeed at Work

Work can feel overwhelming sometimes—deadlines, meetings, and expectations piling up. But here's the good news: when you team up with your boss and coworkers, you can create a workplace setup that works *for you*. Building strong communication and advocating for what you need can turn challenges into wins.

1. Keep Communication Open

Think of it like a work group chat (but way more professional). Regular check-ins with your boss or team ensure everyone's on the same page. Suggest weekly or monthly updates where you can share progress and challenges.

2. Know Your Work Style

If you're better with written instructions than verbal ones, or if breaking tasks into smaller chunks helps, let your boss know. Sharing how you work best isn't complaining; it's setting the stage for success.

3. Advocate for What You Need

If flexible deadlines, noise-canceling headphones, or fewer interruptions during focus time would help, ask for them! Use clear, professional language like:

- "I focus better when I can complete one task at a time. Can we prioritize this approach for me?"
- "Would it be possible to clarify deadlines earlier? That helps me stay organized."

4. Use Tools and Logs to Stay Organized

Work smarter, not harder. Suggest using shared tools like Trello or Google Docs to keep track of projects, progress, and feedback. Keep your own log of accomplishments and challenges—it's a great way to track your growth and show your boss your value.

5. Be Part of the Solution

Workplaces love proactive employees. If something isn't working, propose a fix: "I've noticed this slows me down. Here's an idea to streamline it." This shows you're engaged and invested in doing your best.

Why It's Worth It

When you communicate openly and advocate for what you need, work becomes less stressful and more manageable. It's not about asking for special treatment—it's about creating a setup where you can thrive. With a solid team mindset, you'll meet and crush expectations.

When you get teachers to understand your ADHD brain, everything gets easier. It's not about getting special treatment—it's about getting what you need to succeed. Plus, when your teachers and parents are working together, you'll feel supported from all sides.

So, step up, share what helps you thrive, and turn school into a team sport. You've got this!

9.5 Becoming a Boss at Adulting: Independence Made Easy (and Fun)

Picture this: You wake up, handle your own schedule, make your breakfast, and crush the day without your parents reminding you about a million things. Sounds good, right? Independence isn't just about proving you can do stuff—it's about building confidence, learning life skills, and showing the world (and yourself!) that you've got this. Here's how to start owning your independence, step by step.

Start Small, Win Big

Think of independence like leveling up in a game. You don't tackle the final boss on day one. Start with easy tasks—make your bed, pack your lunch, or keep track of one weekly responsibility like laundry. Nail the small stuff, and soon you'll feel ready to take on bigger challenges, like managing your money or planning your day. Small wins build momentum, so celebrate each one!

Life Skills: Your Power-Ups

Want to be unstoppable? Learn some basic skills that make life easier:

- **Time Management:** Use a planner or an app to map out your day. Bonus tip: schedule breaks so you don't burn out.

- **Cooking Basics:** Master a few easy meals. Trust me, knowing how to make pasta or an epic sandwich is a game changer.

- **Money Smarts:** Start tracking what you spend. Apps like Mint or good old-fashioned budgeting can help you save for the fun stuff.

Problem-Solving Like a Pro

Life throws curveballs (hello, flat tires and forgotten deadlines). The trick? Stay cool and think it through:

1. Identify the problem.
2. Brainstorm solutions (Google is your friend!).
3. Pick the best option and roll with it.

Bonus points if you treat mistakes as learning moments—they're part of the process.

Speak Up for Yourself

You're the expert on *you*, so don't be afraid to let people know what you need. Whether it's asking for clarification at work or suggesting changes at home, speaking up shows you're taking charge. Start small, like choosing what's for dinner, and work your way up to bigger decisions.

Positive Reinforcement: The Secret Sauce

Give yourself props when you crush a goal! Treat yourself to something you love—a favorite snack, extra game time, or a chill night out with friends. Remember, rewards are about progress, not perfection.

It's Okay to Ask for Help

Independence doesn't mean doing everything solo. If you're stuck, reach out to someone you trust. The goal is to grow, not stress out. Plus, teamwork makes the dream work.

You will be surprise how much easier it is to get people to become members of your support team once you asked for help - everyone likes helping another person, especially if it doesn't cost them anything - and let's face it - here they are actually gaining something in return - your friendship or at least respect. Go - give it a try

Why It's Worth It

Independence is not about being perfect; it is about learning and leveling up. The more you take on, the more confident you'll feel. It's not always easy, but every step forward is a win. So start small, embrace the awkward moments, and celebrate every milestone. You've got this—and adulting isn't as scary as it seems!

Chapter 10

Adulting: The Crash Course (With Extra Sass)

Picture this: You're standing at the edge of a diving board, staring into the deep, mysterious waters of adulthood. Exciting? Absolutely. Terrifying? You bet. Transitioning to adult life—especially with ADHD—feels like that nerve-wracking leap. But guess what? You're not doing this solo. Think of this chapter as your personal cheerleader, packed with tips for college, independence, and nailing life. So, ready? Let's cannonball into the deep end together. 🏊 ✨

10.1 Ready for College? Let's Get Those Skills in Shape

College is like upgrading to life's next level, but you need the right gear. Good news: we've got you covered.

Study Smarter, Not Harder

ADHD can make focus feel like spotting Bigfoot, but with the right hacks, it's totally doable. Set up a distraction-free "study throne" (a desk, a library nook—anywhere *but* your bed). Stick to a schedule like your favorite Netflix series—regular, reliable, and with breaks (hello, 10-minute TikTok scroll after every 30 minutes of grinding).

Need help? Campus tutors and academic advisors are basically life cheat codes. They exist to make your goals less stressy and more success-y.

Time, Managed

Adulting = juggling. Deadlines, classes, clubs, and your social life—yikes! Enter digital saviors like Notion, Trello, or Google Calendar. Color-code that chaos and keep your life on track. (Pro tip: Set reminders—because who remembers everything, honestly?)

Social Superpowers: Activate

College is more than books and caffeine-fueled all-nighters; it's about meeting people who *get* you. Join clubs that scream "you"— whether that's improv, gaming, or saving turtles. Nervous about social stuff? Start small. Say "hi" to the person next to you or bond over the weird smell in the dining hall. Professors are just humans with PhDs, so don't be scared to ask questions or crack a (respectful) joke.

10.2 Living Solo: It's a Whole Vibe

Welcome to independence, where frozen pizza counts as a food group (just kidding... kind of). But let's level up your life skills.

Chef It Up

You don't need to be the next Gordon Ramsay. Learn a few easy recipes—think tacos, pasta, or a solid stir-fry. Plan your weekly meals and shop with a list (no, ice cream doesn't count as a list). Bonus: leftovers = tomorrow's lunch.

Tidy Space, Clear Mind

Your room is your sanctuary. Keep it clean-ish. A quick weekly sweep, some organizers, and boom—stress-free vibes.

Self-Care is Key

Don't forget to schedule *you* time. Watch a movie, go for a walk, or vibe out to your favorite playlist. Burnout is *not* invited to this party.

10.3 Workforce Adventures: Let's Do This

Entering the job world can feel like stepping onto a new planet, but don't panic—you're not alone. Let's map this galaxy.

Resume Glow-Up

Your resume? It's your highlight reel. No experience? No problem. Feature those killer group projects, volunteer gigs, or that time you organized a school event and *nailed it*. Tailor each cover letter like a love note to your dream job.

Ace That Interview

Job interviews = your chance to shine. Practice common questions like "What are your strengths?" or "Why do you want this job?" Research the company so you can sprinkle in some insider knowledge. And please, wear pants that aren't sweatpants.

Make Those Connections

Internships and job fairs are where the magic happens. Network like you're collecting Pokémon—each new contact could level up your career. Follow up with a thank-you email to keep the good vibes going.

10.4 Work-Life Balance: The Ultimate Boss Move

Stay Organized AF

Use calendars, to-do lists, and apps to keep your tasks straight. Break big projects into bite-sized pieces, and don't be shy about setting boundaries. Work ends at 5 p.m.? Then your time *starts* at 5:01.

Play Nice at Work

Teamwork makes the dream work. Communicate clearly, listen actively, and handle conflicts like a pro—calmly and with a focus on solutions. Oh, and embrace diversity. Everyone brings something awesome to the table.

Interactive Fun: Meal Planning and Job Prep

Meal Planning Challenge

- Pick a day: Sunday's a vibe.
- Plan your meals: Breakfast, lunch, dinner, snacks—done.
- Shop smart: Stick to the list like it's your manifesto.
- Pro tip: Cook in bulk. Future you will thank you.

Mock Interview Time

- Partner up: Friend, sibling, or maybe a mirror.
- Practice makes perfect: Nail those common questions.
- Feedback FTW: Get notes and tweak till you're unstoppable.

Adulting isn't about knowing everything—it's about figuring things out as you go. Whether you're rocking campus life or crushing it in the workforce, mistakes will happen. What matters is learning, growing, and keeping your sense of humor along the way. You've got this—go out there and show life who's boss.

10.5 Financial Independence: Budget Like a Boss and Manage Your Money

Imagine being able to snag that must-have gadget or plan an epic road trip without your wallet crying for mercy. Financial independence? It's the real glow-up, and it starts with getting your budget in check. Think of it as a money map—it shows you where you are, where you're going, and how to dodge the potholes along the way.

Step 1: Track It or Wreck It

First, figure out what's coming in and going out. Got income from a part-time gig, allowance, or side hustles? Write it all down. Then, list every expense—from rent and tuition to your daily coffee fix and streaming subscriptions. Spoiler alert: those little splurges add up fast. This snapshot shows where your money's disappearing and what you can tweak to keep more in your pocket.

Step 2: Goals Are Gold

What's the dream—saving for your first car, squashing student loans, or building an emergency fund that could save your bacon? Setting clear goals gives your budget a purpose. Rank your priorities and divide your income accordingly. If that shiny new car is top of your list, funnel a chunk of your earnings into a savings account labeled *Vroom Vroom Fund.*

Step 3: Get Techy With It

Budgeting apps are your BFFs here. Download tools like **Mint**, **YNAB (You Need A Budget)**, or **PocketGuard**. They track your spending, set limits, and even hit you with friendly alerts when you're about to overspend (like a digital mom, but cooler). These apps make adulting with money way less stressful.

Save, Invest, Repeat

Now that you're mastering budgeting, it's time to grow your cash flow like a boss.

Build an Emergency Fund

Life happens—flat tires, surprise medical bills, or even a phone that decided to test gravity. An emergency fund with three to six months' worth of living expenses is your financial safety net. Start small and stack it up; future you will thank you.

Level Up with Investing

Got extra cash? Put it to work. Open a high-yield savings account to let your money grow while you sleep. Want to think long-term? Dive into investments—stocks, bonds, or mutual funds. Learn how compound growth works: it's basically free money earning *more* free money. The earlier you start, the bigger the snowball gets.

Dodge the Debt Traps

Debt's like quicksand—easy to fall into, hard to climb out. Here's how to handle it like a pro:

1. **Know Your Debt Types:** Student loans? Lower interest and flexible terms. Credit cards? Higher interest—treat them with caution.

2. **The Avalanche Method:** Tackle high-interest debts first while making minimum payments on others. It's like slaying the biggest dragon first.

3. **Avoid the Predatory Pitfalls:** Payday loans and shady deals might seem like quick fixes, but they're usually traps. Always read the fine print (yes, even the boring parts).

Taxes and Big Adult Purchases

Oh, taxes—like a pop quiz you can't skip. Learn the basics of filing your tax return, and use software or a tax pro if you're lost in the forms.

Thinking of splurging on big buys like a car or your first apartment? Research the costs (hello, insurance and maintenance fees!) and budget for them. Pro tip: always overestimate costs so you're never caught off guard.

Future-Proof Your Wallet

Financial independence is a marathon, not a sprint. Educate yourself on money matters—watch videos, follow finance influencers, or even take a workshop. And if the money world still feels like a foreign language? A financial advisor can help you decode it.

Interactive Challenge: Budget Bootcamp

- **Set a Money Goal:** Pick something you're saving for and set a target amount.

- **Track for a Month:** Write down *every* expense for 30 days. Yes, even that $2 vending machine snack.

- **Analyze Your Spending:** Spot the leaks (bye, daily lattes) and plug them.
- **Celebrate Wins:** Each time you hit a savings milestone, treat yourself—responsibly, of course.

Master these steps, and you'll go from broke to boss in no time. You got this—your bank account will thank you, and so will future-you on that epic, stress-free vacation.

Visual Element: Budgeting Template

Monthly Budget Template

1. **Income:** List all sources of income (part-time job, freelance gigs, allowance).
2. **Fixed Expenses:** List recurring monthly expenses (rent, utilities, transportation).
3. **Variable Expenses:** List expenses that vary each month (groceries, entertainment, dining out).
4. **Savings:** Allocate a portion of your income for savings (emergency fund, investments).
5. **Debt Repayment:** Include payments for any debts (student loans, credit cards).
6. **Total Expenses:** Add up all expenses to ensure they don't exceed your income.
7. **Adjustments:** Review and adjust your budget as needed to stay on track.

By following these steps and using a budgeting template, you can create a clear financial plan that helps you achieve your goals and maintain financial independence. This is just the beginning of your journey towards managing your own money and making smart financial decisions.

Conclusion

Hey, Rockstar!

Wow, what an adventure we've been on together! From unlocking the mysteries of ADHD to mastering time management and building relationships, we've covered a ton of ground. It's been a wild, insightful, and hopefully empowering ride. Ready to wrap it up with some highlights and takeaways? Let's dive in and celebrate how far you've come.

The Highlights Reel

We started by diving headfirst into **understanding ADHD and executive functioning**. First things first, we busted some myths—ADHD isn't about laziness or a lack of motivation. It's about how your amazing brain processes information and tackles challenges. We got science-y, exploring executive functions and why tackling certain tasks can feel like climbing Mount Everest (without a sherpa).

Next, we got into the nitty-gritty of **time management**—because who doesn't want more time to crush their goals *and* binge their favorite shows? From the Pomodoro Technique (hello, productivity ninja) to time blocking, we armed you with hacks to stay focused. Plus, we tackled procrastination with tools like the Two-Minute Rule and even a playlist of motivational jams.

Then came **organization skills**—turning chaos into calm. Whether it was tidying up your space Marie Kondo-style, creating visual reminders, or embracing digital tools, you're ready to get your stuff together—literally and figuratively.

We didn't stop there.

Emotional regulation?

We've got you. Deep breaths, guided meditation, and journaling are your new secret weapons for staying cool under pressure. And we boosted your self-esteem with simple but powerful strategies like positive affirmations, reflecting on your wins, and celebrating *every* victory, no matter how small.

On the social front, we explored **relationships and social skills**. From reading those tricky social cues to owning conversations like a pro, you're set to connect with confidence. We even tackled the digital jungle of social media so you can scroll smarter, not harder.

Then, we broke down decision-making with tools like the Eisenhower Matrix—because adulting is hard, but prioritizing doesn't have to be. Plus, we talked about battling decision fatigue (hint: snacks help).

And because no superhero works alone, we emphasized the role of **supportive parents, teachers, and mentors**. Building a dream team of cheerleaders who *get* you is key to success.

Finally, we geared up for the big leap into adulthood. College prep? Check. Job skills? You're ready. Financial independence? Boom. Living on your own? No sweat (okay, maybe a little, but you've got this).

Key Takeaways

Here's the TL; DR (too long; didn't recap):

1. **Understand your ADHD**: It's not a flaw—it's just a different way of thinking. Knowing how your brain works is step one to thriving.

2. **Crush time management and organization**: Your hacks aren't just survival tools—they're pathways to success.

3. **Build your confidence**: Celebrate those small wins and know that progress is progress, no matter the pace.

4. **Level up your social skills**: Practice makes perfect. Start small, keep trying, and don't sweat the awkward moments.

5. **Embrace the transition to adulthood**: Big responsibilities? Sure. Big rewards? Absolutely. You're more ready than you think.

Take Action

Okay, now the fun part—putting it all into motion! You've got a backpack full of tools, so start by picking just one or two strategies to test out. Maybe it's setting up a Pomodoro timer for your next study session or journaling about your goals. The key? **Start small, stay consistent, and build from there**.

Remember: **progress, not perfection**. If one hack doesn't click, no worries—pivot and try something else. You're building a personalized playbook that works for *you*.

A Final Pep Talk

You are bold, resilient, and capable of more than you realize. ADHD isn't the boss of you—it's just one piece of the unique, unstoppable puzzle that is *you*. With the right tools, mindset, and support system, there's nothing you can't handle.

Keep moving forward, stay curious, and believe in your own magic. You've got this—and I'm here cheering you on every step of the way.

Now go out there and crush it, superstar!

Bonus Chapter

Navigating ADHD with Your Teen: A Guide for Parents

Introduction: Embracing the Journey Together

Living with ADHD is like having a brain that's wired a bit differently—it's unique, vibrant, and sometimes challenging. As parents, it's our mission to be the anchors in this whirlwind, offering support, understanding, and love. This chapter is here to guide you through the intricacies of ADHD, providing practical tips and hacks to create a nurturing environment for your teen.

11.1 Understanding ADHD: More Than Just Hyperactivity

Before diving into strategies, it's crucial to understand ADHD itself. ADHD stands for Attention Deficit Hyperactivity Disorder, which affects focus, self-control, and executive functions. Your teen might experience:

- ☞ Inattention: Struggling to stay focused, easily distracted.

- ☞ Hyperactivity: Constantly moving, fidgeting, or tapping.

☞ Impulsivity: Acting without thinking, interrupting others.

Hack #1: Learn Together - Educate yourself and your teen about ADHD. Watch documentaries, read articles, and join support groups. Knowledge is power, and understanding ADHD helps in tackling it better.

Elaboration:

- ☞ **Watch Together:** Select engaging documentaries or YouTube channels that explain ADHD in a relatable manner. Viewing these together can open up discussions and create a shared understanding.

- ☞ **Read Aloud:** Choose books that explain ADHD in age-appropriate language. Reading together not only imparts knowledge but also strengthens your bond.

- ☞ **Join Communities:** Online forums, local support groups, and social media communities can be a treasure trove of information and support. Sharing experiences with others facing similar challenges can provide comfort and new insights.

11.2 Creating a Structured Environment: The Power of Routine

Teens with ADHD thrive on structure. Creating a predictable daily routine can greatly reduce chaos and anxiety.

Hack #2: Visual Schedules - Use visual schedules with colorful charts or apps to outline daily tasks. This visual aid helps teens keep track of their responsibilities and stay organized.

Elaboration:

- **Personalized Charts:** Involve your teen in creating their visual schedule. Let them choose colors, stickers, or themes that they like. This increases their engagement and ownership of the process.

- **Digital Tools:** Explore apps designed for ADHD that offer customizable reminders and timers. Apps like "Remember the Milk" or "Todoist" can make routine tasks more manageable and less overwhelming.

- **Consistent Check-Ins:** Review the schedule together each evening. This habit not only prepares your teen for the next day but also provides an opportunity to address any concerns or adjustments.

Hack #3: Break Tasks into Smaller Steps - Large tasks can be overwhelming. Break them into smaller, manageable steps and celebrate each accomplishment.

Elaboration:

- **Step-by-Step Lists:** When faced with a big project, create a detailed list of each step. For example, if the task is "Clean the Room," break it down into "Pick up clothes," "Organize desk," "Vacuum floor," etc.

- **Mini Celebrations:** Celebrate each completed step with a small reward or positive reinforcement. It could be a high-five, a favorite snack, or a few minutes of a preferred activity.

- **Visual Progress:** Use charts or apps to visually track progress. This not only keeps your teen motivated but also provides a sense of accomplishment as they see their tasks being completed.

11.3 Fostering Effective Communication: Speak Their Language

Open, empathetic communication is key. ADHD can sometimes lead to misunderstandings or frustrations, so it's essential to foster an environment where your teen feels heard and understood.

Hack #4: Active Listening - Practice active listening. Show empathy, validate their feelings, and avoid interrupting. This builds trust and encourages open dialogue.

Elaboration:

- **Eye Contact and Attention:** Give your full attention when your teen is speaking. Maintain eye contact and avoid distractions like checking your phone.

- **Reflective Responses:** Repeat back what your teen has said to show you understand. For instance, "It sounds like you're feeling frustrated because..."

- **Empathetic Support:** Use phrases like "I understand," "That sounds tough," or "Let's figure this out together." These responses show that you're not only listening but also care about their feelings.

Hack #5: Clear and Concise Instructions - Give clear, concise instructions one step at a time. Avoid overwhelming your teen with too much information at once.

Elaboration:

- **Simplify Instructions:** Break down complex instructions into smaller, manageable steps. For example, instead of saying "Clean your room," say "First, pick up your clothes, then make your bed."

- **Repeat and Confirm:** After giving instructions, ask your teen to repeat them back to ensure understanding. This can prevent miscommunication and frustration.

- **Use Visuals:** Pair verbal instructions with visual aids, like checklists or picture cards, to reinforce what needs to be done.

11.4 Boosting Self-Esteem: Celebrate the Wins

ADHD can sometimes erode self-esteem, but celebrating achievements, no matter how small, can make a big difference.

Hack #6: Positive Reinforcement - Use positive reinforcement to acknowledge effort, not just results. Praise their strengths and progress.

Elaboration:

- **Focus on Effort:** Instead of only celebrating results, acknowledge the effort your teen puts into tasks. Phrases like "I'm proud of how hard you worked on this," can boost their confidence.

- **Specific Praise:** Be specific with your praise. Instead of saying "Good job," say "You did a great job organizing your desk!"

☞ **Reward Systems:** Create a reward system that incentivizes positive behavior and effort. Rewards could be extra screen time, a favorite treat, or a special outing.

Hack #7: Encourage Hobbies and Interests - Help your teen discover and pursue their passions. Engaging in activities they love can boost their confidence and provide a sense of accomplishment.

Elaboration:

☞ **Explore Together:** Spend time exploring different hobbies and interests together. Attend classes, workshops, or community events to find activities that spark their interest.

☞ **Support Their Interests:** Once they find something they love, provide the tools and resources they need to pursue it. Whether it's art supplies, sports equipment, or a musical instrument, your support can make a big difference.

☞ **Celebrate Achievements:** Celebrate milestones and achievements in their hobbies. Display their artwork, attend their performances, or simply express pride in their progress.

11.5 Managing Emotional Regulation: Handling the Ups and Downs

Teens with ADHD often experience intense emotions. Helping them manage these feelings is crucial for their well-being.

Hack #8: Mindfulness and Relaxation Techniques - Introduce mindfulness practices like deep breathing, meditation, or yoga. These techniques can help your teen stay calm and focused.

Elaboration:

- ☞ **Daily Practice:** Integrate mindfulness practices into your daily routine. Start with just a few minutes each day and gradually increase the time as your teen becomes more comfortable.

- ☞ **Guided Resources:** Use guided meditation apps or videos designed for teens. Apps like "Calm" or "Headspace" offer specific programs for managing ADHD.

- ☞ **Join In:** Practice mindfulness together as a family. Not only does this provide support, but it also models the importance of taking time to relax and refocus.

Hack #9: Create a Safe Space - Designate a quiet, safe space where your teen can retreat to when they feel overwhelmed. This can be a cozy corner with their favorite books or music.

Elaboration:

- ☞ **Personal Sanctuary:** Work with your teen to create a personal sanctuary. Let them choose items that make them feel calm and secure, like soft pillows, favorite books, or calming music.

- ☞ **Sensory Tools:** Include sensory tools that help them relax, such as stress balls, fidget spinners, or weighted blankets.

- ☞ **Encourage Use:** Encourage your teen to use their safe space whenever they feel overwhelmed. Remind them that it's okay to take a break and recharge.

11.6 Partnering with Educators: A Team Effort

Your teen's teachers play a significant role in their daily life. Building a strong partnership with them can ensure your teen gets the support they need at school.

Hack #10: Regular Communication - Stay in regular contact with your teen's teachers. Share insights and strategies that work at home, and ask for their input.

Elaboration:

- ☞ **Scheduled Check-Ins:** Schedule regular check-ins with your teen's teachers to discuss their progress and any challenges. This ensures everyone is on the same page and working towards common goals.

- ☞ **Share Strategies:** Share successful strategies that work at home and be open to suggestions from teachers. Collaboration can lead to more effective approaches.

- ☞ **Stay Positive:** Focus on positive aspects during these discussions. Highlight your teen's strengths and progress, while also addressing areas of concern.

Hack #11: Advocate for Accommodations - Work with the school to create an Individualized Education Plan (IEP) or 504 Plan. These plans can provide accommodations like extra time on tests or a quiet space for studying.

Elaboration:

- ☞ **Know Your Rights:** Educate yourself on your teen's rights under educational laws like the Individuals with Disabilities Education Act (IDEA) or Section 504 of the Rehabilitation Act.

- ☞ **Request Evaluations:** If you suspect your teen needs additional support, request evaluations from the school to determine eligibility for an IEP or 504 Plan.

- ☞ **Collaborate on Goals:** Work with the school to set realistic and achievable goals for your teen's educational progress. Ensure that accommodations are tailored to their specific needs.

11.7 Self-Care for Parents: You Matter Too

Parenting a teen with ADHD can be a demanding, and sometimes isolating, experience. The constant vigilance, the need for patience, and the drive to provide the best support for your child can leave little room for your own needs. However, taking care of yourself is not just a luxury; it's a necessity. When you're well-rested, emotionally balanced, and feeling supported, you're in a much better position to help your teen navigate their challenges. This chapter focuses on why self-care is critical and offers practical strategies for finding support and prioritizing your well-being.

Hack #12: Find Support

One of the most powerful tools in your self-care arsenal is a robust support network. Parenting a teen with ADHD can feel like a solitary journey, but many others are walking the same path. Connecting with these parents can provide a sense of community, shared experiences, and valuable advice.

Joining Support Groups

Support groups offer a safe space to share your struggles, triumphs, and everything in between. Here are some ways to find and benefit from support groups:

- ☞ **Local Groups:** Check with your child's school, local community centers, or hospitals to find support groups in your area. These groups often meet regularly and provide face-to-face interaction, which can be incredibly validating.

- ☞ **Online Communities:** Websites like ADDitude, CHADD (Children and Adults with Attention-Deficit/Hyperactivity Disorder), and social media platforms have forums and groups where you can connect with other parents. These platforms allow for flexible participation and can be a lifeline when you're feeling isolated.

- ☞ **Specialized Groups:** Look for groups that cater to specific needs or demographics, such as single parents, parents of teens, or groups focused on co-occurring conditions like anxiety or learning disabilities.

Benefits of Support Groups

- ☞ **Shared Experiences:** Hearing from others who understand your journey can be incredibly comforting. It reassures you that you're not alone and provides practical insights that you might not have considered.

- ☞ **Emotional Support:** Venting frustrations and sharing joys with others who "get it" can reduce feelings of isolation and stress. Knowing there are people who genuinely understand your struggles can be a huge relief.

- ☞ **Practical Advice:** Other parents can offer tried-and-true strategies that have worked for them. Whether it's a new organizational tool, a helpful therapy, or a specific way of communicating with teachers, their advice can be invaluable.

How to Make the Most of Support Groups

- ☞ ***Active Participation:*** Engage actively in discussions, ask questions, and share your experiences. The more you contribute, the more you'll get out of it.

- ☞ ***Be Open and Honest:*** Authenticity fosters trust and deeper connections. Share your highs and lows without fear of judgment.

- ☞ ***Take Initiative:*** If you're not finding the right group, consider starting one. Creating a new group can attract like-minded parents who are also seeking support.

Hack #13: Prioritize Self-Care

Self-care is more than just a buzzword—it's a crucial component of being an effective parent. Prioritizing your well-being helps you maintain the physical and emotional energy needed to support your teen.

- ☞ **Understanding the Importance of Self-Care**

  - ☞ ***Sustained Energy Levels:*** Regular self-care helps maintain your energy levels, preventing burnout. When you're well-rested and emotionally balanced, you're better equipped to handle the demands of parenting.

  - ☞ ***Modeling Behavior:*** By prioritizing self-care, you're teaching your teen the importance of looking after themselves. They learn by watching you, and your actions can encourage them to adopt healthy habits.

  - ☞ ***Stress Reduction:*** Engaging in activities you enjoy can significantly reduce stress levels, improving your overall well-being and ability to cope with challenges.

☞ **Creating a Self-Care Routine**

☞ ***Identify Your Needs:*** Reflect on what activities recharge you. This could be reading, exercising, spending time with friends, or simply having quiet time.

☞ ***Schedule It:*** Treat self-care like any other important appointment. Schedule regular time for these activities and stick to it as much as possible.

☞ ***Start Small:*** If you're new to self-care, start with small changes. Even 10 minutes a day dedicated to something you enjoy can make a significant difference.

11.8 Types of Self-Care

1. Physical Self-Care

☞ ***Exercise:*** Regular physical activity boosts your mood, energy levels, and overall health. Find activities you enjoy, whether it's walking, yoga, dancing, or cycling.

☞ ***Nutrition:*** Eating a balanced diet can affect your energy levels and mood. Prioritize whole foods, and stay hydrated.

☞ ***Sleep:*** Ensure you're getting enough rest. A consistent sleep schedule and a calming bedtime routine can improve sleep quality.

2. Emotional Self-Care

☞ ***Journaling:*** Writing about your thoughts and feelings can be therapeutic. It helps you process emotions and gain insights into your experiences.

- ☞ ***Therapy:*** Consider seeking professional help if you're feeling overwhelmed. Therapy provides a safe space to explore your emotions and develop coping strategies.

- ☞ ***Mindfulness and Meditation:*** Practices like mindfulness and meditation can help you stay present and manage stress. Even a few minutes a day can be beneficial.

3. Social Self-Care

- ☞ ***Connect with Friends and Family:*** Spending time with loved ones can boost your mood and provide a support system.

- ☞ ***Set Boundaries:*** Learn to say no to additional responsibilities that may overextend you. It's okay to prioritize your well-being.

- ☞ ***Engage in Hobbies:*** Pursue activities that bring you joy and relaxation. Whether it's gardening, painting, or playing an instrument, hobbies provide a creative outlet.

4. Mental Self-Care

- ☞ ***Continued Learning:*** Engage your mind with activities like reading, puzzles, or taking up a new hobby. Lifelong learning keeps your brain active and engaged.

- ☞ ***Limit Media Consumption:*** Be mindful of your media consumption, especially news. Too much exposure to negative information can increase stress and anxiety.

- ☞ ***Practice Gratitude:*** Regularly acknowledging things you're grateful for can improve your overall outlook and mental health.

Incorporating Self-Care into Your Daily Life

- *Morning Routine:* Start your day with a few minutes of something that brings you joy or peace, such as stretching, drinking a cup of tea, or listening to music.

- *Micro-Breaks:* Throughout your day, take short breaks to do something relaxing. Even a 5-minute walk or a few deep breaths can help reset your mind.

- *Evening Wind-Down:* End your day with a calming activity. This could be reading a book, taking a bath, or practicing meditation. It helps signal to your body that it's time to relax and prepare for sleep.

Overcoming Barriers to Self-Care

- *Guilt:* Parents often feel guilty taking time for themselves. Remember that self-care is not selfish—it's essential. Taking care of yourself means you're better able to care for your teen.

- *Time Constraints:* Busy schedules can make self-care feel impossible. Prioritize and protect your self-care time, even if it means starting small.

- *Finding Support:* Enlist the help of family or friends to take over some responsibilities for a while. This can free up time for you to focus on self-care.

Creating a Supportive Environment

- **Communicate Your Needs:** Let your family know how important self-care is to you. Explain that by taking care of yourself, you can be more present and supportive for them.

- ☞ **Involve Your Teen:** Encourage your teen to participate in self-care activities with you. This not only models healthy behavior but also strengthens your bond.

- ☞ **Set Realistic Expectations:** Understand that self-care doesn't have to be perfect. Some days will be harder than others to find time, and that's okay. The goal is to make it a regular practice, not a source of additional stress.

Developing a Self-Care Plan

- ☞ *Assess Your Current Routine:* Take stock of how you're currently spending your time. Identify areas where you can incorporate self-care.

- ☞ *Set Goals:* Define what self-care means to you and set achievable goals. For example, aim to read for 15 minutes before bed or take a walk every morning.

- ☞ *Track Progress:* Keep a self-care journal to track your activities and how they make you feel. This can help you see the positive impact over time and stay motivated.

The Ripple Effect of Self-Care

When parents prioritize self-care, the benefits ripple outwards. You become more patient, more empathetic, and better equipped to handle the complexities of parenting a teen with ADHD. Your teen also learns from your example, understanding the importance of taking care of themselves. This holistic approach fosters a healthier, happier family dynamic.

Conclusion: You Matter Too

Supporting a teen with ADHD is a journey filled with unique challenges and incredible rewards. As you navigate this path, remember that taking care of yourself is a vital part of being the best parent you can be. By finding support and prioritizing self-care, you not only enhance your well-being but also create a positive, nurturing environment for your teen. Embrace the journey, take time for yourself, and know that you are doing an amazing job.

By understanding ADHD, creating a structured environment, fostering effective communication, boosting self-esteem, managing emotions, partnering with educators, and prioritizing self-care, you can help your teen thrive. Remember, you're not alone in this journey—support, resources, and your unconditional love make all the difference.

I hope this chapter provides a helpful, supportive guide for you and your parents navigating ADHD with you. Remember, everyone is unique, and it's about finding what works best for your family. Happy reading and best of luck on this journey together!

References

📖 The neurobiological basis of ADHD | Italian Journal of Pediatrics
https://ijponline.biomedcentral.com/articles/10.1186/1824-7288-36-79

📖 What Is Executive Function? 7 Deficits Tied to ADHD
https://www.additudemag.com/7-executive-function-deficits-linked-to-adhd/

📖 Common ADHD Myths - Child Mind Institute
https://childmind.org/article/common-adhd-myths/

📖 Academic and Social Functioning Associated with Attention ...
https://www.ncbi.nlm.nih.gov/pmc/articles/PMC5831167/

📖 Pomodoro Technique for ADHD: Why it Helps & How ...
https://www.choosingtherapy.com/pomodoro-technique-adhd/

📖 Time Blocking: ADHD Time Management Technique
https://www.tiimoapp.com/blog/time-blocking-for-adhders

📖 3 to-do list apps that actually work with ADHD
https://zapier.com/blog/adhd-to-do-list/

- 📖 9 Tips for Creating a Routine for Adults with ADHD https://psychcentral.com/adhd/9-tips-for-creating-a-routine-for-adults-with-adhd

- 📖 How to Stop Procrastinating by Using the "2-Minute Rule" https://jamesclear.com/how-to-stop-procrastinating

- 📖 Instant Gratification and the ADHD Brain: How to Navigate a ... https://www.hamptontutors.com/blog-feed/2017/11/19/instant-gratification-and-the-adhd-brain-how-to-navigate-a-culture-of-immediacy-tpg4z-2bjrj#:~:text=There%20are%20several%20methods%20of,pleasures%20while%20staying%20task%2Ddirected.

- 📖 Will Eating the Frog Boost Your Productivity? https://www.shimmer.care/blog/adhd-productivity-strategies-eat-the-frog

- 📖 13 Productivity Playlists to Center and Focus ADHD Brains https://www.additudemag.com/focus-music-for-adhd-brains/

- 📖 The Many Mental Benefits of Decluttering https://www.psychologytoday.com/us/blog/the-resilient-brain/202302/the-many-mental-benefits-of-decluttering

- 📖 Visual Aids: A Vital Tool for Students with ADHD https://medium.com/@ckaczeducation/visual-aids-a-vital-tool-for-students-with-adhd-bbf3a9eb5b25

- 📖 Time Management Apps for Teens with ADHD https://www.additudemag.com/time-management-apps-teens-adhd-productivity-focus/

- 📖 The ADHD Adult's Definitive Guide to Weekly Review and ... https://marlacummins.com/the-adhd-adults-guide-to-the-weekly-review/

📖 Mindfulness Exercises for Teens with ADHD
https://www.additudemag.com/slideshows/mindfulness-exercises-for-teens-adhd/

📖 Best Mindfulness and Meditation Apps for Teens
https://evolvetreatment.com/blog/mindfulness-apps-teens/

📖 Journaling for ADHD: Benefits, Tips, and Prompts - Healthline
https://www.healthline.com/health/adhd/journaling-for-adhd#:~:text=Journaling%20can%20be%20a%20valuable,and%20promote%20better%20time%20management.

📖 The Stress Bucket – A model for understanding stress
https://www.hey.nhs.uk/wp/wp-content/uploads/2020/08/OHC_StressBucket.pdf

📖 How to Build Self Confidence in Teens with ADHD
https://www.additudemag.com/how-to-build-self-confidence-adhd-teens/

📖 26 Positive Affirmations for ADHD to Promote Success
https://www.livingopenhearted.com/post/adhd-affirmations#:~:text=ADHD%20affirmations%20can%20help%20us,to%20when%20things%20get%20challenging.

📖 Why It's Important to Celebrate Small Successes
https://www.psychologytoday.com/us/blog/1-2-3-adhd/202111/why-its-important-to-celebrate-small-successes

📖 Personal Stories of Teens Living with ADHD
https://chadd.org/for-teens/personal-stories-of-teens-living-with-adhd/

📖 How ADHD May Be Impacting Your Child's Social Skills
...

https://www.foothillsacademy.org/community/articles/adhd-social-skills

- 📖 Easy Conversation Starters: Socializing with ADHD
  https://www.additudemag.com/easy-conversation-starters/

- 📖 Teens with ADHD: friends \u0026 friendships
  https://raisingchildren.net.au/teens/development/adhd/friends-friendships-teenagers-adhd#:~:text=Teenagers%20with%20ADHD%20might%20need,reminders%20to%20contact%20their%20friends.

- 📖 Navigating the Challenges of Social Media for ...
  https://www.childnexus.com/blog/article/navigating-the-challenges-of-social-media-for-neurodivergent-youth-65464eb50ea4f

- 📖 Overcoming Decision Fatigue in ADHD
  https://www.psychologytoday.com/us/blog/changing-the-narrative-on-adhd/202405/overcoming-decision-fatigue-in-adhd

- 📖 Teaching the Eisenhower Matrix to ADHD Students - ADDitude https://www.additudemag.com/eisenhower-matrix-how-to-prioritize-plan-adhd/

- 📖 ADHD and Decision Making: Symptoms, Tips, and More
  https://psychcentral.com/adhd/adults-adhd-tips-to-make-good-decisions

- 📖 Time Management for Teens and Tweens With ADHD
  https://www.webmd.com/add-adhd/childhood-adhd/teens-tweens-adhd-time-management

- 📖 Communication Skills for Kids with ADHD: 11 Helpful ...
  https://www.additudemag.com/communication-skills-for-kids-adhd/

- 📖 Creating a Supportive Home Environment for Children with ...
  https://www.artiegatelytherapy.com/post/creating-a-supportive-home-environment-for-children-with-adhd

- 📖 ADHD in the Classroom: Helping Children Succeed ...
  https://www.cdc.gov/adhd/treatment/classroom.html

- 📖 Positive Reinforcement in Children and Adolescents with ADHD
  https://www.pathwaysneuropsychology.com/positive-reinforcement-in-children-and-adolescents-with-adhd/#:~:text=Positive%20reinforcement%20includes%20providing%20verbal,the%20behavior%20will%20be%20repeated.

- 📖 10 Study Tips for Children and Teens with ADHD
  https://nextstep4adhd.com/10-study-tips-for-children-and-teens-with-adhd/

- 📖 8 Time Management Tips for Students - Harvard Summer School https://summer.harvard.edu/blog/8-time-management-tips-for-students/

- 📖 Money Smart for Young Adults
  https://www.fdic.gov/consumer-resource-center/money-smart-young-adults

- 📖 5 Strategies for Neurodivergence Success in the Workplace
  https://www.rethinkcare.com/resources/neurodivergence-workplace-actionable-strategies-success/